Glorious
GOURD
Decorating

Glorious
GOURD
Decorating

Mickey Baskett

Sterling Publishing Co., Inc.
New York

PROLIFIC IMPRESSIONS PRODUCTION STAFF:

Editor in Chief: Mickey Baskett
Copy Editor: Phyllis Mueller
Graphics: Dianne Miller, Karen Turpin
Styling: Kirsten Jones
Photography: Jerry Mucklow, Pat Molnar, Joel Tressler
Administration: Jim Baskett

Library of Congress Cataloging-in-Publication Data Available

Baskett, Mickey.
    Glorious gourd decorating / Mickey Baskett.
        p. cm.
    ISBN 0-8069-6945-8
    1. Gourd craft. I. Title.
TT873.5.B35 2003
745.5--dc21

2003002684

10 9 8 7 6 5 4 3 2 1

Published by Sterling Publishing Co., Inc.
387 Park Avenue South, New York, N.Y. 10016

© 2003 by Prolific Impressions, Inc.

Produced by Prolific Impressions, Inc.
160 South Candler St., Decatur, GA 30030

Distributed in Canada by Sterling Publishing
c/o Canadian Manda Group, One Atlantic Avenue, Suite 105
Toronto, Ontario, Canada M6K 3E7
Distributed in Great Britain by Chrysalis Books
64 Brewery Road, London N7 9NT, England
Distributed in Australia by Capricorn Link (Australia) Pty. Ltd.
P.O. Box 704, Windsor, NSW 2756 Australia

Printed in the USA
All rights reserved
Sterling ISBN 0-8069-6945-8

PRODUCT ACKNOWLEDGEMENT

Plaid Enterprises, Inc.
www.plaidonline.com
A special thanks for supplying FolkArt Acrylic Paints for many of the decorative painting projects.

Walnut Hollow
www.walnuthollow.com
Supplier of woodburning tools and supplies.

Artist Acknowledgments

Many, many thanks to these talented gourd artists who supplied photographs and projects for this book. They are listed here in alphabetical order, and contact information is provided for many of them.

Latana Jan Bernier
3499 Burnley Station Road
Barboursville, VA 22923
ljkbinva@aol.com

Dic Bonsett
4391 Highway 61
Two Harbors, MN 55616
dic@bonsett.com

Francie Broadie
1313 Old Town N Dr.
Indianapolis, IN 46260
broadie@in-motion.net

Aurelia Conway
Hummingbird Hill
10285 S. 500 E.
Elizabethton, IN 47232
www.hummingbdhill.com

Patty Cox
4025 Linden Ave.
Ft. Worth, TX 76107

Emily Dillard
7243 W. 92nd St.
Zionsville, IN 46077

Jeanie Dixon
Gourds by Jeanie
6305 W. Argent St.
Pasco, WA 99301
www.gourdsbyjeanie.com

Susan Ebel
Oh My Gourdness!
2641 Cowley Way
San Diego, CA 92110
smebel@aol.com

Marla Helton
3875 W. 250 N.
Greencastle, IN 46135
www.geocities.com/
serendipitygourd

Julie Jurow
3604 Fairbanks Way
Antioch, CA 94509
juliejurow@attbi.com

Rowena Philbeck
5377 Rye School Rd.
Bryan, TX 77807
Rowena@taz.tamu.edu

Raymond Powers
Creekside Crafts
P.O. Box 1062
Ojai, CA 93024
raypows@ojai.net

Carolyn J. Rushton
1387 N. 800 E.
Glenwood, IN 46133
carolrushton@hotmail.com

Marcia Sairanen
Twining Vines
P.O. Box 5061
El Dorado Hills, CA 95762
www.twiningvines.
homestead.com

Robin McBride Scott
4222 East Co. Rd. 750 N
New Castle, IN 47362
www.honoringtheancestors.com

Sharon Seprodi
618 E. Beech Street
Sullivan, IN 47882
www.alteredgourds.com

Rebecca Shelly
1901 Berry Street
Lemon Grove, CA 91945
www.naturespottery.com

Laraine Short
Laraine's Creative Corner
275 Ranch Rd.
Ponte Vedra, FL 32082
aGourdPainter@aol.com

Marguerite Smith
30075 Alta Mira Ln.
Valley Center, CA 92082
www.lasting-memories.net

W. Jayne Stanley
Gourdsket® Vessel Company, Inc.
P.O. Box 1413
Evergreen, CO 80437
www.gourdsket.com

Elinor Tenney
Oh My Gourdness!
31886 Ritson Rd.
Escondido, CA 92026
bgtenney@aol.com

Betty Valle
803 Woodlyn Dr. South
Cincinnati, OH 45230

Denny Wainscott
4128 W Co. Rd. 200 N
Frankfort, IN 46041
www.morningdewgourds.com

TABLE OF CONTENTS

Artist: W. Jayne Stanley

These lovely gourds were created from kettle gourds stained with nature based pigments. Jayne's unique reverse coiling technique with western pine needles and waxed linen fibers finish the top of the vessels.
Photo by Azad.

THE GOURD AS ART

Introduction by Aurelia Conway

GOURDS ARE A GIFT FROM NATURE. Long before Michelangelo picked up a brush, ancient cultures were marking drinking gourds with charcoal sticks for identification. Gourds are magical, wondrous, and practical. Through the ages they have been tools, ornaments, spiritual icons, entertainment, and – always – a form of creative expression.

The hardshelled gourds used for this art form are members of the *Lagenaria siceraria* botanical family, which includes pumpkins, melons, and squash. While growing, a gourd is 90% water, but when the stem stops feeding the gourd, drying begins. After a few months the water evaporates through the skin, eventually leaving a hard shell. This drying process produces an outer mold that, when removed, exposes a smooth, hard surface. Often the mold leaves permanent marbling on the gourd, adding to its appeal.

A collection of gourds – representing a variety of shapes and sizes – awaits the artist's touch.
Photo by Susan Ebel and Elinor Tenney

Very young gourds are eaten for food in some parts of the world, and in some cultures various parts of the gourd plant have been used as medicine, but hardshelled gourds are not usually considered edible. Their most common uses throughout history have been as containers and surfaces for decoration. They can be cut and shaped to make bowls, boxes, baskets, pitchers, and dippers, and they have wonderful, smooth, three-dimensional surfaces that can be carved, burned, waxed, varnished, and colored.

This section of the book provides an overview of the history of gourd art and introduces some outstanding gourd artists. You will see a range of sizes, from small gourds used for jewelry to a large gourd that's the base for a coffee table, and a variety of inspirations – ancient pottery, natural materials, animals, found objects, and Asian art, among others.

Continued on next page

Artist: Denny Wainscott

The technique of these carved and colored gourds is done by first drawing the designs on the gourds with pencil and then woodburning the designs. Areas of the design are then carved away with a paragraver, which is like a dentist drill. The gourds are stained with a combination of leather dyes and wood stain. When all the stain and dye is dry, the pieces are sprayed with an acrylic sealer.

Artist: Marla Helton

Above: Dyed gourd decorated with dried philodendron, pods, and jute.

Right: Dyed gourd woven with waxed linen thread in a twill weave.

Historians believe gourds are one of the few plant species found around the globe in prehistoric times. The earliest seeds and fragments were discovered in Peru and date to at least 10,000 B.C. Primitive humans valued the hardshelled gourd for its functional uses. It's believed early Africans not only used gourds to make eating utensils and musical instruments, but also as floats for fishing nets, giving rise to the theory that some of those gourds may have floated across the seas to other lands. This would be an amazing feat, considering the gourd might have survived for a year in salt water and still produced viable seeds.

Artist: W. Jayne Stanley

This piece entitled "The Drifter" was crated from a basketball gourd which was "textured" and put through several layers of nature based pigments. The top is coiled with handspun wool, silk, waxed linen and pine needles. The embellishments include seeds, gemstones, glass beads, and a driftwood handle.
Photo by Azad

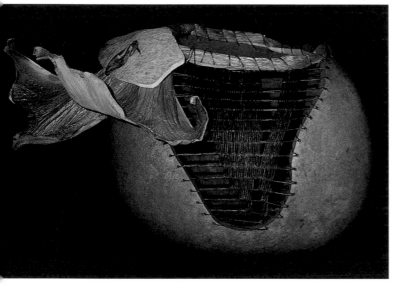

Artist: Rowena Philbeck

Tenerife weaving on stained gourd, using waxed linen and philodendron sheath and wooden embellishments.

In Japan, gourds were considered talismans of good luck, and the great shogun warrior Hideyoshi Toyotomi charged into battle with a gourd atop of his flagpole. The Chinese carried sacred crickets in decorated gourd cages that symbolized prosperity and fertility because it was believed that gourds held the future and the wishes of the gods.

In Mexican folklore, gourds are considered houses for the spirits and the way the spirits of ancestors return. In Hawaii, the gourd represents the universe and gourd drums ("Ipu") are still made today for religious ceremonies. In North America, Southwestern Native Americans treasured gourds as water vessels, especially the canteen gourd.

Artist: Dic Bonsett

Cannonball gourd grown in Indiana, decorated with pyrography and wood stains.

Over time, people began to embellish and decorate gourds – perhaps the earliest examples were gourd "baskets," dyed with native plants and embellished with weeds and plant fibers. There are hundreds of varieties of gourds – their names usually describe either the gourd's shape (kettle, bushel, apple, penguin, egg) or common function (dipper, canteen, bottle), to name a few. No two gourds are ever exactly alike.

Continued on next page

Artist: Denny Wainscott

"Healing Spirits" gourd is created with pyrography and carving using a paragraver, which is like a dentist drill. The design is colored with leather dyes and wood stains. After the dyes and stains are dry, the piece is sprayed with an acrylic sealer. The turquoise dot is then added by inserting crushed turquoise and an epoxy mix into a carved out area.

Today's gourd art shows the imaginative possibilities of working with a three-dimensional surface. Each design offers artists the opportunity to develop techniques and incorporate the unique shape of each gourd. Artists have adapted ancient techniques to produce musical instruments, baskets, eating utensils, birdhouses, and ornaments, and modern tools and resources have given rise to new artistic styles. Some of the decorative techniques and unique uses for the gourds include:

- **Pyrography** – using a wood burning tool to engrave images on the gourd surface. Also known as woodburning.
- **Pyro-engraving** – using a fine tool to cut intricate designs.
- **Staining and dyeing** – coloring the gourd surface with natural or synthetic mediums.
- **Painting** can be easily done on a gourd since it offers a smooth hard surface. Acrylics, oils, and watercolors all work well on gourds.

- **Inlay** is the process of cutting or carving out areas of the gourd and inserting materials such as precious stones or emu egg pieces.
- **Sculpting** is usually done by cutting away portions of the gourd, leaving outlines of shapes or designs.
- **Pen and ink images** are created by outlining the natural marbling on a gourd or creating an original design. It is as simple as it sounds – pen and ink are used to ink the design. Many times dyes are used to add color.
- **Decoupage** works well on the smooth surface of the gourd. Pressed ferns, flowers, or paper can be bonded to the surface using decoupage finishes and then embellished with a variety of other artistic techniques.
- **Basketry** often embellishes a gourd. Natural reeds, grasses, pine needles or other natural objects are woven around the top of the gourd or into cut-out areas following the

Continued on next page

Artist: W. Jayne Stanley

These gourds were created from club gourds that were stained with nature-based pigments. They are coiled with handspun wool, silk, sea grass, and pine needles. The embellishments include gemstones, and glass beads.
Photo by Azad

Artist: Marla Helton

Dyed gourd woven with Danish cord, using a coil weave.

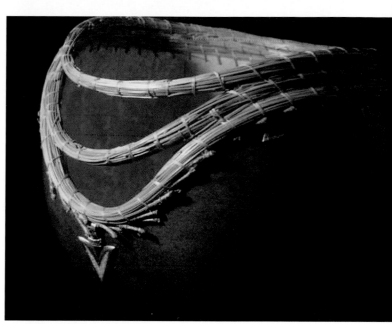

Artist: Latana Bernier

"Formal Attire" 12" bowl with pine needle coiling and a sterling and turquoise arrowhead.

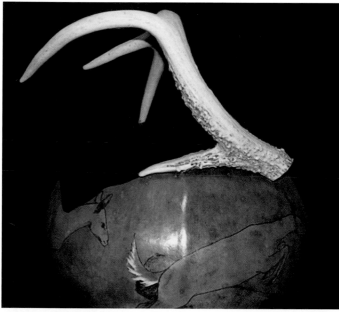

Artist: Latana Bernier

"The Buck Stops Here" Pyro-engraved, carved, and etched 12" gourd basket colored with paste wax. The deer's antler forms the handle.

Artist: Lantana Bernier

"Paradox" 4" bowl, pyro-engraved and stained, with 4" white pine needle coiling.

native Indian traditions. Often the surface of the gourds, inside and out, is dyed, stained, or left natural.

- **Jewelry** is a unique way to use the hard shells of the dried gourds. All types of techniques are used to make the jewelry; including beading, pyrography, inlays, carving, etc.
- **Vases and bowls** are popular items to make from a gourd because the gourd is so hard and impervious to liquid.

The vessels are created by cutting open a gourd, cleaning out the inside and then decorating it with a variety of techniques.

- **Abstract sculptures** are fun to create with gourds. Artists look at the actual shape of the gourd and then decide on a structure of an object that it might suggest. In some cases, objects are glued onto the gourd for added effects.

Artist: Julie Jurow

"Rocketbuster Boots" Kettle gourd, 14" tall, 10-1/2" wide, pyro-engraved and stained with leather dyes. Photos show 2 sides.

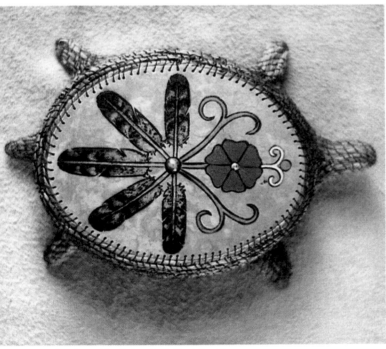

Artist: Robin McBride Scott

Sweetgrass and gourd turtle. Part of a bushel gourd was woodburned, decorated with paint and beads and stitched sweetgrass.

Artist: W. Jayne Stanley

"Curves of the Imagination" vessel was created from a giant bushel gourd that was stained with nature based pigments. An asymmetrical cut gives the ancient technique of pine needle/waxed linen coiling a contemporary feel.

Gourds have survived the ages. They are magical and wondrous and yet practical. Through the ages, they have offered mankind tools for comfort, spiritual icons, entertainment, and a form of creative expression. As William Shakespeare said, "One touch of nature makes the whole world kin." Tracing the history of gourd art throughout the ancient and modern world, one can see how this unique bond transcends time.

Artist: Julie Jurow

"Eagle Ponies" A basketball gourd, 10-1/2" tall and 11" wide. The background is painted with acrylic paint; the ponies were colored with oil pastels.

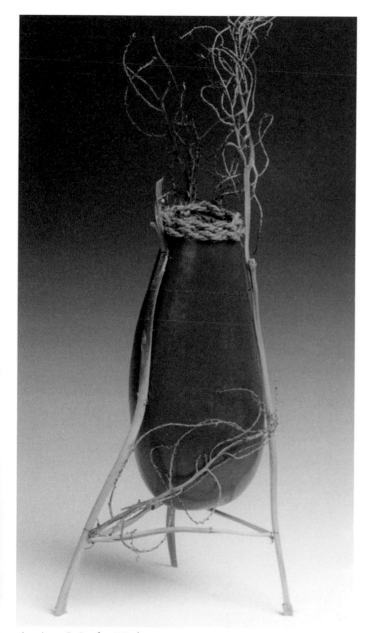

Artist: Marla Helton

Dyed gourd with legs of palm, woven with coir.

Artist: Marla Helton

Dyed gourd woven with dracena.

Artist: Emily Dillard

This intricate woodburned, lidded vessel is colored with oil pencil. All species of animals peek out from vegetation that is created with real pressed flowers and ferns that are decoupaged to the surface. Inside (the lid can be removed), is painted with acrylic paint and decorated with more decoupaged pressed flowers and ferns.

Artist: Marguerite Smith

"Tiger Eyes" is a woodburned design that is colored with a combination of paint and stain.

Artist: Marguerite Smith

"Proud but Gentle Pride" is a lovely example of woodburning. The design is colored with paint and stain.

Pictured above:

Artist: Denny Wainscott

"Turquoise Vessel" is woodburned and carved with a paragraver. Turquoise inlays are created with a crushed turquoise and epoxy mix that, after drying, is sanded with progressively finer grit papers. The final sanding is with 2000 grit wet paper. The gourd is colored with leather dyes and wood stains and finished with an acrylic spray sealer.

Pictured far left:

Artist: Sharon Seprodi

"Vessel" A penguin gourd, used upside down, is cut, stained and accented with cork and polymer clay.

Pictured immediate left:

Artist: Robin McBride Scott

Bell gourds form the head and the small rattle (it actually works!) of this Native American-influenced doll. The long part of a dipper gourd is used for the body. The figure, 8-1/2" tall, is decorated with acrylic paint, horsehair, feathers, and beads.

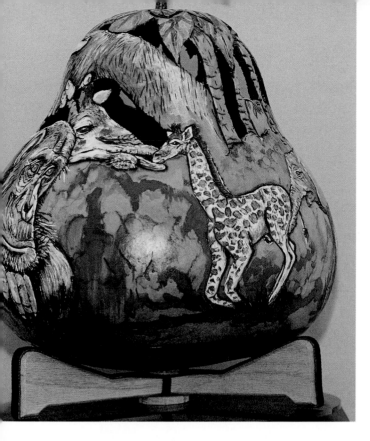

Artist:
Marguerite Smith

"Helping Hands" is a fine example of the combination of woodburning and painting. Notice that some of the area of the gourd is carved away for added dimension.

GOURDS AS MUSICAL INSTRUMENTS

MUSICAL INSTRUMENTS CAN BE CREATED from gourds of all sizes and shapes, from the smallest rattles to the largest drums. Percussion instruments utilize the beautiful tones of the hollowed out gourd.

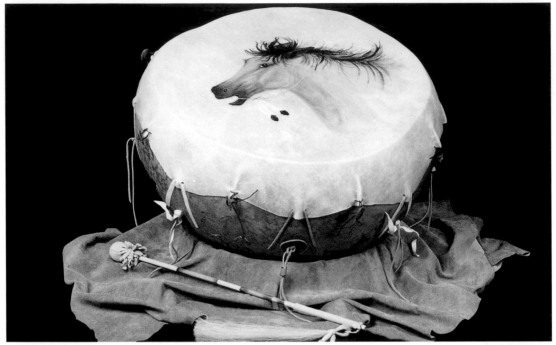

Artist: Carolyn Rushton

Gourd drum. Made from a bushel gourd that has a cowhide drumhead with woodburning and oil painting.

Artist: Raymond Powers

"Whirl" Ceremonial gourd rattle, hand carved, woodburned, decorated with pottery images from Cucuteni, Romania (3800-3600 B.C.), feathers, and dyed cowhide and fitted with a wooden handle. It is made from a 6" canteen gourd.

GOURDS AS JEWELRY

GOURD JEWELRY IS MADE BY ARTISTS of all mediums and includes beading, pyrography, and inlays. Pictured below are two beaded necklaces featuring tiny gourds.

Artist: Raymond Powers

"Waterbird" Ceremonial gourd rattle, hand carved, woodburned, decorated with pottery images from Minoa, Crete, (1400 B.C.), peacock and pheasant feathers, and dyed cowhide and fitted with a wooden handle. It is made from a 6" canteen gourd.

Artist: Francie Broadie

Artist: Francie Broadie

GOURD WHIMSY & FANTASY

GOURDS CAN BE THE STARTING POINT and inspiration for a variety of whimsical, fanciful objects. Designs are created by looking at the shape of the gourd and deciding what structure or thing it might suggest. Embellishments may be glued on the gourd for added effects.

Pictured right:
Artist: Rebecca Shelly

Gourd teapot, made from a Chinese bottle gourd, painted and decorated with a variety of found (recycled) objects.

Pictured bottom right:
Artist: Marcia Sairanen

Gourd basket decorated with fruits and filled with smaller gourds of various shapes colored with leather dyes, colored pencils, and acrylic paint to resemble fruits. The basket was cut with a jigsaw; detailing was done by pyrography.

Pictured bottom left:
Artist: Mary Denton

Halloween luminary. After the bottom was cut away and the gourd was cleaned, a simple jack o' lantern face was cut. The luminary can be placed over electric mini lights or a low-wattage night light to illuminate.

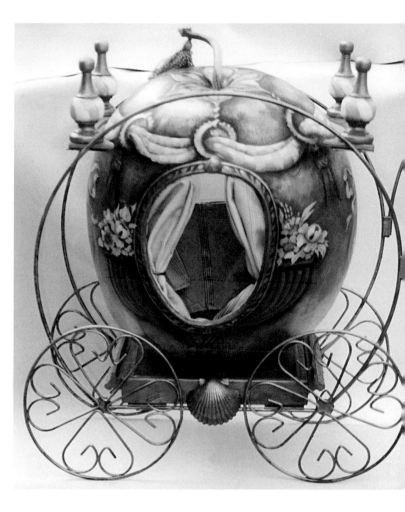

Artist: Emily Dillard

Birdhouse. The gourd is painted with white acrylic paint and given a crackle finish. Shingles and flowers are constructed from gourd seeds, which are painted with acrylic paint.

Artists: Susan Ebel and Elinor Tenney of Oh My Gourdness!

Cinderella's Carriage is a painted gourd with a carriage constructed of wire.

Cinderella's Carriage, before painting and decorating. When it was given to the artist, the gourd was 30 years old.

Artist: Jeanie Dixon

Giant Gourd Coffee Table, painted with acrylic paints and hand-rubbed with a durable, moisture-resistant sealer.

Artist: Emily Dillard

Leather-dyed club gourd with an all-natural arrangement.

GOURDS
WITH AN
ASIAN LOOK

Artist: Emily Dillard

Oriental double bowl. The gourds are stained with leather dye and decorated with acrylic painted designs. The lid on the top bowl can be removed; one gourd bowl sits atop the other, the smaller forming a lid for the larger one beneath. The handle is made from reed.

Artist: Emily Dillard

Leather-dyed Oriental Bowl. Can be made food-safe by coating the inside with a "salad bowl finish" sealer.

Artist: Emily Dillard

Oriental double bowl. The gourds are stained with leather dye. The acrylic-paint medallions are decorated with a gold paint pen.

CHOOSING & PREPARING GOURDS

Types of Gourds

Gourds come in a variety of sizes and shapes, and their common names are generally descriptive of their shapes or what they might be used for. Here are examples of some shapes that are popular with gourd artists.

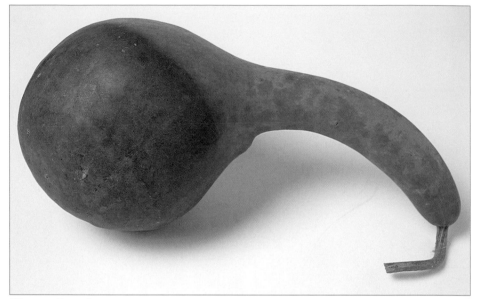

Egg Gourd

Dipper Gourd

Bushel Basket Gourd

Cannon Ball Gourd

Apple Gourd

Canteen Gourd

Tobacco Box Gourd

Cave Man's Club Gourd

Chinese Bottle Gourd

Kettle or Martin Gourd

Growing Gourds

With minimal effort and some garden space, it's possible to grow a crop of gourds in a variety of shapes and sizes. If you want to grow a particular type or size of gourd, select seeds from a reputable nursery or seed producer. Because gourds are hybrids and each seed in a gourd is pollinated from a different pollen grain, it can be impossible to predict what the product of a particular seed will be unless care has been taken to raise single species and lessen the risk of cross-pollination. (Of course, the surprises of cross-pollination are part of what makes gourds so interesting.)

Gourds need a warm, sunny location with plenty of room, fertile soil, and regular watering. Plant in hills (six to eight seeds to a hill) or in rows spaced eight to ten feet apart in good soil enriched with rotted manure or compost or fertilizer after danger of frost is past. Most gourds (except the very large ones) can be grown on a trellis or an arbor. The necks of gourds grown on an arbor or trellis are typically straight; necks of gourds grown on the ground are usually curvy. Trellising also keeps gourds from becoming flat on one side.

The seeds will germinate in a week to ten days. You can speed up germination by soaking the seeds in water for three or four days before planting; the seeds also can be started indoors in peat pots and transplanted after two weeks. Because gourds are native to warm areas, they grow most vigorously in warm, sunny weather.

A group of green gourds before drying.

The gourd's white flowers are pollinated by flying insects (often at night) and can be pollinated by hand. The same insects and diseases that affect other members of the same plant family (like winter squashes and pumpkins) in your area may attack your gourds. Seek advice from more experienced growers or the appropriate agency for specific growing information suitable to where you live.

Maturity may take as long as 140 days. General cultivation advice includes watering thoroughly every week in dry weather, top dressing them in midsummer to feed them, and leaving the gourds on the vine until the tendril next to the stem is dead. To harvest, cut the gourds from the vine with pruning shears. (Long stems are considered attractive.) Don't pick up the gourd by the stem – it can break off.

Drying Gourds

If you grow your own gourds, harvest them after a killing frost when the plant's vegetation has died. Gourds allowed to stay on the vine are usually of better quality than gourds that are cut off the vine early.

You can bring the gourds inside to dry, put them in a shed on wooden-slatted pallets, or leave them in the garden.

The freezing and thawing of winter will not hurt the gourds. If you are allergic to molds, it's recommended that you dry them outside. Additionally, gourds emit a distinctive odor as they dry that many people find unpleasant. If your gourds are outdoors, you won't notice the smell.

To dry them inside, place gourds in a well-ventilated space, arranged so that they are not touching. Indoors, drying takes four months or longer.

Curing outdoors can take one to six months, depending on the size and type of the gourd. The outer skin hardens in one to two weeks; internal drying takes longer and varies. For best results, turn the gourds occasionally as they dry, checking for soft spots or signs of damage. If the gourd becomes soft or spongy that means it is rotting – there's nothing to do but throw it out. Gourds are 90 percent water, and as the water evaporates through the skin and the cut end of the stem, a mold forms. (See the following pages for how to clean a gourd.) As long as the gourd does not have soft spots or evidence of surface damage, it will be perfectly good to use even if it looks moldy.

Be sure the gourd is completely dry before you begin to cut or decorate it. A fully dried gourd is light in weight, and when you shake it you will hear the seeds rattle.

COMMON-SENSE PRECAUTIONS

The interior pulp of a gourd and the dust that results from scraping, cutting, and sanding gourds can be toxic and irritating to the eyes, nose, and mouth and cause breathing difficulties. As you work, keep these precautions in mind:

- Work outside. Do the cleaning and cutting outdoors. The fresh air will do you good, and you won't have to clean up a lot of dust and debris when you're finished.

- Wear a mask. The dust masks sold in hardware stores can protect your nose and mouth; if you know you are sensitive to dust, you may want to wear a filtration mask. Look for them in shops that sell woodworking equipment, at crafts stores, and in mail order catalogs.

- Wear eye protection. Glasses or goggles will protect you from dust and splashes.

- Wear gloves. Put on a pair of plastic or rubber gloves to protect your hands and wear a shirt with long sleeves, particularly if your skin is sensitive or if you are allergic to dust.

Pictured at left: A cleaned gourd, left, and an uncleaned gourd, right. The cleaned gourd has a smooth surface that is ready to decorate. The mold on the outer skin of an uncleaned gourd may be white or black or both. Sometimes the mold leaves marks on the gourd that will not scrub off. If you're painting the gourd and want a uniform background for the design, you can apply a tan acrylic paint to block the mold markings. Many people consider the mold markings attractive and part of the gourd's appeal.

Cleaning Gourds

Cleaning gourds is messy, but not difficult. The first step is cleaning the moldy skin on the outside. After the outside has been cleaned and is thoroughly dry, the gourd may be cut and cleaned on the inside.

CLEANING THE OUTSIDE

Underneath the moldy skin is a wonderful smooth surface. **Do not** drill holes in the gourd or cut the gourd before cleaning the outside.

1. Let your gourd soak in warm water for 10 minutes. Use a dishpan or a bucket for soaking. *Option:* Add automatic dishwasher detergent to the soaking water.
2. Use a metal dish scouring pad to scrub away all of the moldy outer skin. Keep a wire brush handy for tough spots and for scrubbing around the stem. Be sure there are no cracks or soft places.
3. Dip the cleaned gourd in a mild solution of chlorine bleach and water. (This will kill any remaining mold spores.) Dry in the sun.

CLEANING THE INSIDE

If you are going to cut open the gourd to use as a bowl, basket, or vase, you will need to clean the inside before painting or decorating. Refer to the instructions on how to cut a gourd before cleaning the inside.

1. Fill the cut gourd with warm water. Let stand 20 minutes.
2. Scrape out the inside with a sharp tool, such as a wood chisel. A large prying bent flathead screwdriver or a wire brush will work, too. Some artists use the flap wheel on a drill for difficult gourds. Repeat the soaking and scraping processes as needed until the gourd is cleaned. Let dry thoroughly.
3. Sand the inside to smooth.

TOOLS FOR CLEANING INSIDE GOURDS

Pictured left to right: Sandpaper, a prying flathead screwdriver, a wood chisel, a wire brush.

Scrubbing the gourd

Sanding the inside of a cut gourd.

Tip: If you see bubbles when you are cleaning the outside, there is a hole! Clean the gourd quickly, and set it in the sun or in an oven to dry. Shake. When the inside is dry, you'll hear the seeds rattling again.

Cutting Dried Gourds

CUTTING TOOLS

There are a number of tools you can use to cut a gourd. A standard jigsaw or saber saw will work quite well, but a miniature jigsaw with a variable speed motor (which allows you to vary the speed of the cut, giving you more control) is worth the additional cost if you are going to work with a lot of gourds.

You can also use a craft knife to cut gourds (use a sawtooth blade) and to make a hole for inserting a saw blade. Be sure to use a fresh, sharp blade in the knife for smooth cuts.

The object you are creating determines the tool you'll use:

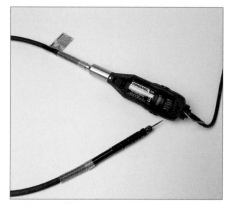

A Dremel Tool

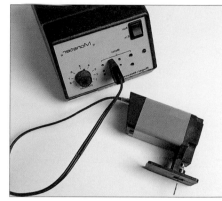

A variable speed miniature jigsaw

To cut a vase, use a band saw, miniature jigsaw, coping saw, jigsaw, saber saw, or hand saw.

To cut a bowl, use a Dremel tool with a diamond cutter, a miniature jigsaw, or a standard jigsaw or saber saw.

To cut a birdhouse, use a drill or drill press equipped with a hole saw and a 1/8" drill bit.

HOW TO CUT YOUR GOURD

Cutting with a Miniature Jigsaw: Use a pencil to draw guidelines for cutting. Hold the gourd with one hand, insert the saw blade in a slit that was cut with a craft knife, and begin cutting. Follow your pencil line as you work around the gourd.

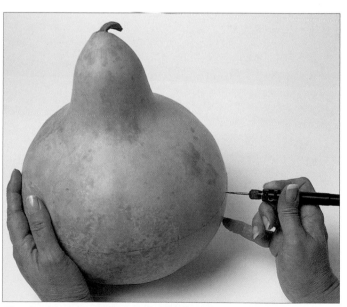

Cutting with a Dremel Tool: Use a pencil to draw guidelines for cutting. Place the tip of the cutter on the line and begin cutting. For a smooth, fine edge, the diamond cutting bit works best. Move the tip along your pencil line. Using a flex shaft extension on the end of the Dremel Tool makes it easier to handle.

FOR BOWLS

Place the gourd on a flat surface and draw a line around it. You will want the line to be the same distance from the table up (not from the stem down). Cut on this line with a mini jigsaw, a craft knife with a saw blade, or a Dremel tool.

```
┌─────────────────────────────────────────┐
│                 T I P S                  │
├─────────────────────────────────────────┤
│                                          │
│ • Try using a jar as a guide for making  │
│   the line: Rest a pencil on top of a    │
│   jar and move it around the gourd.      │
│   You can change the jar height          │
│   according to how tall your gourd is    │
│   and how deep you want your bowl.        │
│                                          │
│ • For a scalloped edge bowl, measure     │
│   the line you've drawn and divide by    │
│   ten. Make a circle template the        │
│   diameter of the result. Use the        │
│   template to draw above the line, then  │
│   below the line to get a nice even edge.│
│                                          │
└─────────────────────────────────────────┘
```

FOR BIRDHOUSES

Birdhouses need entrance holes (for the birds to get in) and holes in the bottom for draining away water. **Cutting the Entrance Hole:** To place the hole, position the pattern and transfer or use a template (any round object that's the size of the hole you want to make).

A hole saw circle cutter

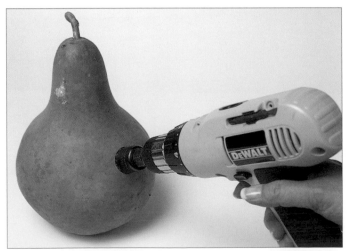

Cutting an entrance hole with a hole saw on a drill. Align the cutter with the marked hole. Hold the gourd tightly.

The easiest way to cut an entrance hole for a birdhouse is to use a hole saw circle cutter, which can be found at any hardware store. This is a metal tubular saw that fits on a drill press or drill. (It's most frequently used for cutting holes in doors for doorknobs.) Attaching the circle cutter to a drill press allows you to steady the gourd as it is being cut. If you use a standard drill, be careful that the circle cutter doesn't skip, since you are not working on a flat surface.

Another way to cut the hole is to use a Dremel Tool with a diamond cutter. Mark the placement of the hole with a pencil, place the tip of the tool on your pencil mark, and cut around the perimeter of the hole.

MAKING DRAINAGE HOLES & HOLES FOR HANGING WIRE

Use a 1/8" drill bit to drill drainage holes and holes for attaching hanging wire.

Drilling holes for drainage. Turn gourd upside down and drill three or four holes.

```
┌─────────────────────────────────────────┐
│           BIRDHOUSE HOLE SIZES           │
├─────────────────────────────────────────┤
│                                          │
│ The diameter of the hole determines the  │
│ type of bird your birdhouse will attract: │
│              House Wren: 1"              │
│            Chickadee: 1-1/8"            │
│ Tufted Titmouse, Nuthatch, or Bluebird:  │
│                  1-1/4"                  │
│           Carolina Wren: 1-1/2"          │
│          Martin or Flicker: 2-1/2"        │
│                                          │
└─────────────────────────────────────────┘
```

PAINTING GOURDS

GOURDS offer wonderful, smooth surfaces to paint. Often, the gourd's shape is the inspiration for a painted design; other times, they may be used as a three-dimensional canvas for landscapes or motifs. They can be cut to form bowls, vases, and pitchers and their shapes can be the basis for a variety of holiday decorations, including jack o' lanterns and Christmas ornaments, that can be used year after year.

Be sure your gourd is completely dry before you start to paint it. If you try to paint a gourd that is not completely dry, it will become moldy.

Because each gourd is unique, there are considerations for placing designs:

• Whether the gourd will sit or hang can determine how the design should be placed. Align the design according to how you will use the gourd.

• Because no two gourds are exactly alike in shape or size, you may have to reduce or enlarge a pattern to fit a particular gourd.

• Since a gourd does not have a uniform shape, a pattern with a repeat or a border may need adjustments. Make sure the design looks attractive from the front of the gourd – the back is less noticeable.

PREPARATION: Before painting, fill all holes with wood filler; then wet the top of the filler with water to smooth. Let dry. Sand any bumps. Some artists recommend sanding all over the gourd with extra fine sandpaper before painting to ensure a smooth surface.

Painting Supplies

PAINT: Gourds can be painted with acrylic or oil paints; acrylic paints are by far more convenient because they are easy to clean up with soap and water and they dry quickly. Acrylic craft paints, which come in plastic squeeze bottles and are available at crafts and hardware stores in a huge array of colors, are used for painting most of the projects in this book.

BRUSHES: Using good quality brushes – of the right type and size – is very important. Each type of brush has its own function.

Shaders or "bright" brushes are flat brushes with a fine chisel edge. They are used for basecoating, for various types of strokes, and for floating highlights or shading. It's best to have at least one small, one medium, and one large.

Round brushes usually have longer bristles and are placed in a round ferrule. They are used for basecoating and many strokes.

Liner or script brushes are round brushes with fewer bristles but longer hairs.

They are pointed on the end for fine detail work. They come in several lengths.

Filbert brushes are round brushes with flat ferrules. The unusual shape allows for easy leaf strokes and other strokework.

Angular shading brushes are similar to the flat or "bright" brushes, except the chisel bristles are cut at an angle. Angular shaders are used for floating highlights or shading in small or tight areas, utilizing the pointed angle.

Deerfoot or stippler brushes have shorter bristles and are tightly packed into a round ferrule. They are usually used for painting fur or pouncing color for foliage.

FINISHES: Varnishes penetrate the gourd skin, making the painted surface very durable. Seal with brush-on or spray varnish. You can choose gloss, satin, or matte sheen. A sealer made for outdoor use that has UV blockers will protect the paint from sun fading and is a good idea for birdhouses and other outdoor applications.

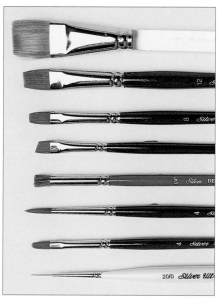

Pictured above top to bottom: Wash brush, #12 flat brush, #8 flat brush, #8 angular shader, 1/4" deerfoot brush, #4 round brush, #4 filbert, 20/0 liner brush.

Base Painting

Some projects will instruct you to paint the entire surface of the gourd or certain areas before transferring the pattern. This is called base painting. It is not necessary to seal a gourd before painting.

Use a dampened large flat or bright brush to paint the entire surface. Stroke the brush over the surface to distribute

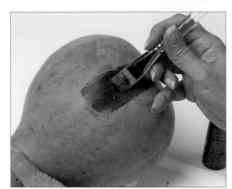
Base painting

the paint evenly, making sure you do not leave ridges. Go back over the surface while the paint is wet to remove any irregularities. Depending upon the color, you may have to apply two coats. (This is usually specified in the instructions if it's necessary.) Let the first coat dry before applying the second coat. If you don't, you can lift off the first coat.

Transferring Patterns

There are two basic methods for transferring a pattern to a gourd – using clear plastic wrap or cardboard templates. Because each gourd is unique, there are considerations:

• Whether the gourd will sit or hang can determine how the design should be placed, so make that decision first. Align the design according to how you will use the gourd.

• Because no two gourds are exactly alike in shape or size, you may have to reduce or enlarge a pattern to fit a particular gourd.

• Since a gourd does not have a uniform shape, a pattern with a repeat or a border may need adjustments. Make sure the design is balanced in the front – the back is less noticeable.

• If the instructions call for base painting, do this before transferring the design. Small design elements in the foreground may have to be transferred after other painting is done.

USING CLEAR PLASTIC WRAP

Use this technique if you have a large all-over pattern that is not symmetrical and the pattern needs to wrap around the gourd.

1. Place a piece of clear plastic wrap over the pattern. Trace the major pattern elements with a fine tip permanent marker.
2. Place the wrap on the gourd, aligning it to the way the gourd will sit or hang, depending upon your purpose.
3. Slide a piece of graphite paper under the wrap and retrace your lines. Remove the graphite paper and plastic wrap, and you are ready to paint. After painting, erase the

Transferring a pattern using clear plastic wrap

transferred lines before varnishing.

USING CARDBOARD TEMPLATES

This method works especially well if you have small elements such as windows or doors and the positioning needs to be determined in relation to the size and shape of the gourd. This method allows you to experiment with the positioning of design elements before marking the gourd.

1. Trace the pattern on a piece of tracing paper.
2. Transfer the design to a piece of poster board by sliding a piece of graphite under the tracing paper. Transfer the design shapes to the poster board.
3. Cut out the design shapes from the poster board with scissors or a craft knife, creating the templates.
4. Position the templates on the gourd. Trace around each template with a pencil or fine tip permanent marker. Fill in details after the template shapes are aligned and traced.

USING TRACING PAPER

Use this method if you have a small design element – such as a small flower design – that will be positioned on a relatively flat area of the gourd.

1. Trace the pattern on a piece of tracing paper.
2. Position the tracing on the gourd and tape in place on one or two sides.
3. Slide a piece of transfer or graphite paper under the tracing, graphite side down.
4. Re-trace the pattern, transferring the design to the gourd.

WOODBURNING TECHNIQUES

PYROGRAPHY OR PYRO-ENGRAVING – more commonly known as woodburning – is a time-honored art and craft of creating a design with a heated tool on a surface. Woodburning a design results in a warm, rustic look that works wonderfully with both traditional and contemporary interiors. With a simple heating tool that has a sharp point, any design can be engraved on a gourd – almost as easily as using a pencil on paper.

The following pages provide information on the tools, equipment, surfaces, and coloring and staining supplies you'll need to create your woodburned gourd projects. These supplies are available in crafts, hobby, or art supply shops, or on the Internet.

Woodburning Tool

All the projects in this section were completed using a solid shaft woodburning tool with interchangeable points. Three points were used: the flow point, the mini-flow point, and the shading point. The solid shaft woodburner is packaged with a wire holder and at least one point. A good starter point is the flow point, which has a rounded end and moves freely over the surface to produce a line.

Several point styles are available for specific purposes, and points can be purchased as an assortment that includes the most common ones. (The point most frequently supplied with the burner is called a universal point because it is intended as an all-purpose tool. However, it is probably the most difficult point to master and should be set aside until you become familiar with the other points.)

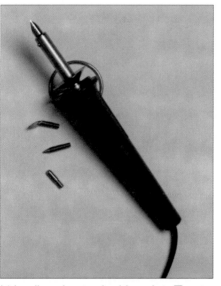

Woodburning tool with points. Top to bottom, the points pictured are the shading point, the mini flow point, and the flow point.

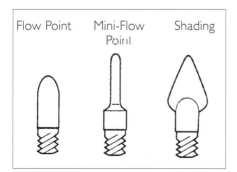

Once you have learned to use the three recommended points, you may wish to experiment with some of the others or even try using a variable temperature-wire tip woodburning system. These systems are much more costly than the solid shaft tool and are designed for much more intricate detail work.

Cautions: Remember that the woodburning point will reach a temperature of 950 to over 1000 degrees Fahrenheit. It is perfectly safe to use as long as certain safety measures are taken, and the rules are followed. Children under 12 should not be allowed to use a woodburner without close adult supervision at all times, and a junior woodburning tool is recommended for them. It only reaches a temperature of between 600 to 750 degrees Fahrenheit.

Woodburning Supplies

WORKSPACE SET-UP SUPPLIES

In addition to the woodburning tool and the points, you'll need a few additional items when setting up your work space:

A 4" **ceramic tile**, for taping down the wire holder for the woodburner. The tile is heavy enough so it won't move around on the work surface, and it is heatproof.

A **container**, such as a metal lid, a glass dish, or ceramic plate, to place the hot burner points in until they cool. When removed from the hot woodburner, the points retain their heat for a couple of minutes, so they need to be treated with care.

A pair of **needlenose pliers** with plastic or rubber-coated handles, for removing the hot point from the woodburner and replacing it with a different one. After changing a hot point, the pliers retain the heat for a couple of minutes, so it's a good idea to rest the metal part of the pliers on the points container until cool.

A folded **piece of sandpaper**, for cleaning carbon buildup from the hot point.

Aluminum foil or other heat-resistant material, to cover your work surface.

SUPPLIES FOR COLORING

Acrylic craft paints, which are available pre-mixed in a huge range of colors and glittering metallics, can be used to color and accent designs.

Stains and glazes, both water- or oil-based, can be used to color gourds. You can buy pre-mixed stains and glazes or mix your own using **neutral glazing medium** (a transparent liquid or gel) and acrylic paint. The medium's long drying time allows you to blot and rub colors for a variety of effects. An 8-oz. bottle or jar is enough for several projects. Acrylic craft paints, pre-mixed stains and glazes, and glazing medium are available at crafts and art supply stores.

Permanent markers are great for coloring gourds. They are easy to control and the color is transparent.

Leather dyes, which come in a range of beautiful colors, are pigments dissolved

Painting and glazing supplies

in a solvent (usually alcohol or mineral spirits). They can be used as overall stains or to accent designs. Apply them with a foam brush, a dauber, or a bristle brush. Find them at crafts stores and shoe repair shops.

Silk fabric dyes can be used to color design elements. They don't work as well as leather dyes on large areas. Find them at crafts stores.

Oil color pencils are constructed of an oil pigment contained in a wax base. The pencils come in a large array of colors and can be layered and blended. Because these pencils are made of wax, they are as comfortable and familiar as the crayons you probably used as a child.

The pencils need to be kept sharp, so you'll need an **electric or battery-operated pencil sharpener**. Sometimes, pencil artists hone the points with a razor-sharp knife to prevent waste, but unless you're coloring a very large surface, this isn't necessary.

OTHER SUPPLIES

• Use **recycled plastic containers** with lids for mixing stains and glazes – you can mix more stain than you need immediately, then put on the lid and save it for a few days. The lids are also good for mixing colors. A **glass jar** can also be used for mixing.

• Recycled cotton athletic socks make terrific **rags** for blotting and rubbing down stains and glazes, as do old, soft terrycloth towels. Rags should be clean and free of lint.

• It's handy to have a half-and-half **ink/pencil eraser**. The smooth white plastic end is excellent for removing lead pencil or oil pencil without damaging the surface. When you need more eraser power, the gray end of the eraser, which has a gritty substance imbedded in it, acts as an abrasive to remove difficult marks. If you can't find a half-and-half eraser, choose a white plastic one and use very fine grit **sandpaper** for persistent marks.

• Use **cotton swabs** to move the oil pencil wax around on the surface to blend the colors and make them smooth.

Oil pencils and supplies

FINISHES

- **Spray-on matte acrylic sealer** is used for sealing the insides of gourds and sealing oil pencil coloring. Matte sealer spray can be used as a final sealer on pieces that won't get heavy use.

- **Brush-on acrylic varnish**, available in matte, satin, and gloss sheens, is used to finish pieces that get heavy use and as a sealer to mask areas of designs to protect them from stains or glazes. Apply varnish with a flat, soft bristle brush or sponge brush.

The Woodburning Technique

PREPARING THE WOODBURNER

To set up your woodburner, tape the wire holder that comes with it to a ceramic tile. Then tape the tile to the work surface to secure it. Use needlenose pliers to insert a point into the end of the woodburner shaft. Tighten to secure. Rest the woodburner on the wire holder and plug it in. It will take four or five minutes to heat fully. Whenever the burner is not in use, rest it on the wire holder. Unplug it when you finish the woodburning portion of your design.

Preparing the woodburner

CHANGING POINTS

While the woodburner is hot, it is possible to change points by using rubber or plastic-handled needlenose pliers. **Never** touch any metal part of the woodburner with your fingers. **Always** use pliers. Firmly grasp the point with the tip of the pliers holding the plastic shaft of the woodburner in the other hand. Twist the point counter-clockwise, remove it, and immediately place the hot point in a glass, tin, or ceramic receptacle. The point will retain its heat for several minutes, and the receptacle will get hot. Pick up your chosen point with the pliers and insert it into the shaft, tightening securely.

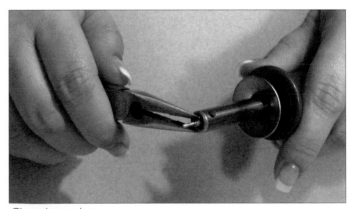

Changing points

CLEANING THE POINT

While you work with the woodburner, you will probably accumulate debris on the point. Keep a square of medium grit sandpaper handy. Occasionally wipe the point across the sandpaper to clean off the debris. Check the cooled points occasionally and sand them as needed to keep them bright and shiny.

Cleaning the point

Techniques

To achieve the darkest, deepest burn, hold the wood-burner as you would a pen or pencil, and move at about half the speed you would use when writing or drawing. While burning, keep the point moving. If you stop, lift the point from the surface to avoid dark blotches, spots, and unwanted burns. The darkness of the burn is controlled by the length of time the point is touching the surface, not by pushing the point into the gourd.

Most of the time, you will want to maintain a solid, even, flowing line. The best way to achieve this is to hold the burner lightly, turning the gourd as you go so that you are pulling the line toward you rather than pushing it away from you. For small skips in the line, re-burn the area with short "chicken scratching" or sketching movements.

Practice on a scrap of gourd before starting any projects. You might practice by first penciling, then burning your name and the date. Touch the point to the surface slowly and lightly. Write very slowly, letting the point flow across the surface. Lift the point from the surface when you end a line to avoid making a darker dot.

If you accidentally make a small burning error, you may be able to sand it away with fine grit sandpaper, then erase

Hold the burner like you would hold a brush or pencil, letting it rest naturally in your hand. Do not touch any of the metal parts.

remaining marks with an ink eraser. Larger errors are permanent, and you will need to find a way to incorporate them into your design.

CHOOSING THE POINT TO USE

Use these guidelines to help you choose which of the three points to use for different effects.

- Flow Point: The flow point is good for outlining designs and creating line patterns.

- Shading Point: The shading point is held with the leaf-shaped bottom of the point flat against the surface while the point is moved in small circles. It can also be dragged slowly along the outside edge of an object or design to create a shadow effect. Practice to discover the precise angle that produces the best deep, dark color for your own personal touch.

- Mini-Flow Point: The mini-flow point makes a line just a bit narrower than the flow point. It is good for adding details such as dots and stippling. To make even round dots, the tool is held perpendicular to the surface and the point is touched to the surface, then lifted again. Holding the point to the surface longer will create larger dots. If you touch and lift very quickly, you will create a stippled look.

The
Projects

GOURDS INSPIRE CREATIVITY. The wonderful shapes, the smooth surfaces begging to be decorated, and the hard, wood-like composition make the dried gourd a perfect surface for artful creations. Within these pages, you will see the gourd made into bowls, birdhouses, vases, purses, sculptures, and more. The surface of the dried gourds can be cut, woodburned, painted, dyed, stained, carved, decoupaged, and decorated with three-dimensional items such as beads, fiber and more. Whatever your favorite technique, you are sure to find a gourd project you wish to make – or one that will inspire you to create your own design.

DRIED FLOWER BOWL
DECOUPAGE TECHNIQUE

By Emily Dillard

SUPPLIES

Decorating Materials:

A clean gourd, any size

Decoupage medium

Dried pressed flowers and foliage

Optional: Paint or leather dye or colored tissue paper (for coloring the surface of the gourd), colored pencils, colored ink, acrylic paint, watercolors, oil pencils (for enhancing flower colors)

Acrylic spray sealer

Tools & Equipment:

Scissors (for trimming)

Wax paper

INSTRUCTIONS

1. Leave the gourd its natural color and spray with a thin coat of acrylic sealer *or* apply a background color, using leather dye, paint, or decoupaged tissue paper. Allow to dry thoroughly.
2. Choose and arrange the flowers and foliage you want to use.
3. Working one piece at a time, place a piece of plant material on a piece of wax paper and apply decoupage medium to the back of the material (the side that will be against the gourd).
4. Quickly place the piece on the gourd, positioning it according to your design plan. *Tip:* You will be able to slide the piece around for a short time. If it won't move easily, don't force it; instead, revise your design.
5. Brush decoupage medium on the piece until the plant material is covered and the edges are sealed.
6. Repeat steps 3 and 4 until all plant material is adhered to the gourd. Allow to dry according to manufacturer's instructions, until transparent.
7. Apply additional coats of decoupage medium until the surface feels smooth. Allow each coat to dry before applying the next.
8. *Optional:* Spray with acrylic sealer. Let dry.
9. *Optional:* If colors eventually fade, you may touch up the colors with colored pencils, colored ink, acrylic paint thinned with water, watercolors, or oil pencils. ❏

OTHER OPTIONS FOR DECOUPAGE

- Use only leaves (no flowers) to create a variety of designs:
  Cover the gourd with leaves for color and texture. Use whole leaves, cutout shapes, or torn pieces.
  Use leaves as shapes for making designs. Remove the stems and place them as mirror images, for example, or cut them apart to form designs like starbursts or flowers.

- For a leathery look, apply sheets of tissue paper. Overlap them, and don't worry if they wrinkle. Allow to dry, then rub with shoe polish.

- Create designs from motifs cut from paper or thin fabric. Use transparent glazes, stains, or dyes to color.

ROSE BASKET
CUT & PAINTED

By Susan Ebel

SUPPLIES

Decorating Materials:

Kettle gourd, 8-10" diameter (Find a gourd that sits flat *or* sand the bottom to flatten so your gourd sits upright.)

Acrylic craft paint:

Black green
Blush flesh
Burnt umber
Cadmium yellow
Dark green
Forest green
Medium flesh
Medium green
Dark Rose
Mint julep
Napthol red
Payne's gray
Pumpkin
Raw sienna
Warm white
White

Finishing wax

Optional: Flocking medium (for the inside)

Tools & Equipment:

Chalk pencil

Cutting tools

Brushes:

Flats - #12, miscellaneous smaller flats
Liner
Filberts - #4, #6

PREPARE

1. Draw the outline on the gourd of the upper part of the basket design to be cut away. Use a chalk pencil to do this. There is no pattern, and the instructions are very general because each gourd has its own personality and size. The size of your gourd will determine the size of your basket and roses. Set your gourd on a flat surface and sketch on a horizontal line totally around the gourd, about 1/2 way up the side. Then sketch the width you want for the handle.

2. Cut out the basket shape. *Tip:* It is best to cut first, then paint because you always run the risk of cutting a bit off the design and it is easier to change the design before you paint.

3. Paint the entire gourd very loosely with forest green, adding some dark green towards the bottom. Let dry.

4. Sketch the placement of the roses. Each rose will start with a circle. Use the chalk pencil to draw large circles to represent where the roses will be placed. Each circle should be 2-1/2" or 3", depending upon the size of your gourd. With the chalk pencil, identify the direction each will be facing.

PAINT THE DESIGN

Roses:

These roses are fantasy flowers, painted in an impressionistic manner. Each flower has a color theme, but feel free to throw in touches of other colors for interest. Paint the background roses first. Let dry, then paint the foreground roses. Here are the color themes:

Pink rose - Base with medium flesh. Paint throat with dark rose. Paint loose petals with blush flesh. Highlight petals with blush flesh + white. Shade with dark rose.

Red rose - Base with napthol red. Paint throat with dark rose. Paint loose petals with napthol red + white. Highlight with napthol red + more white. Shade with dark rose.

Dark rose - Base with dark rose. Paint throat with Payne's gray. Paint loose petals with dark rose + napthol red. Highlight petals with blush flesh + white. Shade with dark rose.

Yellow rose - Base with pumpkin. Paint throat with dark rose. Paint loose petals with cadmium yellow + pumpkin. Highlight petals with cadmium yellow + white. Shade with dark rose.

Continued on page 44

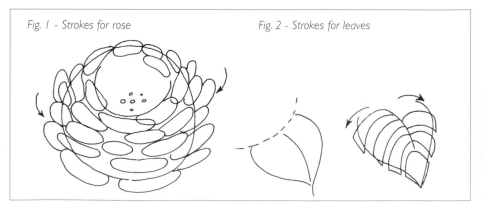

Fig. 1 - Strokes for rose   Fig. 2 - Strokes for leaves

Continued from page 42

Here's how:

1. Base the shape of the rose in the color specified.
2. Add a oval bowl in the "throat" color, and use that color to side-load the bottom edge of the bowl.
3. Paint the petals, using a filbert or round brush and comma strokes that vary in length and size. They should swirl around the throat of the rose. The petals at the bottom of the rose should be longest. Leave some space between them so the basecoat shows through. Let the petals extend beyond the base-coated area. See Fig. 1.
4. Apply the highlight color primarily on the left front edge. Add a touch of highlight on the opposite top right edge.
5. Go back and darken the petals of the background roses a bit where they emerge from under another rose.
6. For the centers, add dots of dark green in the throat. Place tiny dots of cadmium yellow on top of the green dots.

Vines:

1. Base with raw sienna.
2. Shade with burnt umber.
3. Highlight with winter white.

Leaves & Stems:

1. Base the leaves loosely with medium green.
2. Use sideloaded dark green to paint the shadows where flowers or other leaves overlap.
3. Use a smaller flat brush with medium green + some mint julep to shape the leaves, working on half the leaf at a time. See Fig. 2.
4. As needed, re-establish veins with dark green.
5. Add stems with dark green, using a liner brush. Let dry.

FINISH

1. Wax the outside of the gourd.
2. *Option:* Coat the inside with wax, a flocking medium, or paint. If you paint, using very watery paint will make the color flow more evenly. ❏

Illustration for Painting Pink Rose

Illustration for Painting Yellow Rose

Pansy Basket Patterns

Enlarge @200% for actual size.

See page 46 for project instructions.

Straight lines indicate the basket handle.

Fig. 1 - Cutting & Basketweave Diagram

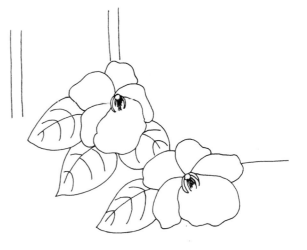

PANSY BASKET
CUT & PAINTED

By Susan Ebel

Pattern appears on page 45.

SUPPLIES

Decorating Materials:

Kettle gourd

Acrylic craft paint:

Black green
Black
Burnt umber
Dark green
Dioxazine purple
Honey brown
Lavender
Medium green
Mint julep
Primary yellow
Pumpkin
True blue
White
Winter blue
Yellow ochre

Glazing medium

Varnish *or* finishing wax

Tools & Equipment:

Chalk pencil

Mini craft saw

Brushes:

Liner
Flats - 1/2", 3/4", #12
Flat shaders - #12, #8, #4
Rake or old scruffy brush

PREPARE

Cut:

1. Using Fig. 1 as a guide, mark the basket shape on the gourd with a chalk pencil.
2. Using the photo as a guide for placement, transfer the flower patterns to the basket.
3. Cut the gourd to form a basket, cutting around the outlines of the flowers, using a mini craft saw.

Mark the Basketweave Design:

1. Choose the largest brush you can easily use. (I used a #12.) Each row will be the width of your brush.
2. Set the gourd on a flat surface. If it doesn't sit securely, sand the bottom to flatten it.
3. Draw concentric rings the width of your brush around your gourd, parallel to the top cut edge of the basket, using a chalk pencil.
4. To make the vertical guidelines, place a pushpin at the bottom center of the gourd and stretch a rubberband over it and up and over the stem. Loosely draw along the side of the rubber band, move it over, and draw again. (This aids in achieving the bulging look of the weave.) The width of the weave should loosely correspond to the width of your brush above and below the midpoint. At the "equator," the squares will be wider than your brush. At the "poles," they will be a bit narrower.
5. Mark a border along each edge of the handle, then mark the "lazy S" strokes between the borders. See Fig. 1.

PAINT THE BASKET

Base:

1. Load a #12 flat brush with honey brown. Tip one side of the brush in burnt umber and the opposite side in yellow ochre. Blend on a palette. Paint the basketweave, alternating vertical strokes with the dark edge on the left and horizontal strokes with the dark edge on the top. Use the photo and Fig. 1 as guides.
   • With chalk, mark the area covered by the flowers and leaves. Don't paint the basket underneath those areas.
   • The colors will blend with the natural color of the gourd; if the skin shows it will add depth.
   • You may need to reload and repaint some squares.
   • A streaky look is natural.
2. Highlight the weave using a rake brush or an old scruffy brush. Use yellow ochre and light-heavier-light pressure on your stroke to concentrate the color in the center of each square.

Handle:

1. Paint the handle with the same three colors used for the basket base, painting horizontally along the wavy pattern and straight along the borders, using a triple-loaded brush.
2. Highlight with yellow ochre.

Continued on page 48

Continued from page 46

PAINT THE FLOWERS

Leaves:

1. Base the leaves with dark green. Use the same color to paint the edge of the gourd where the leaf is on the cut edge.
2. Loosely highlight the leaves, using a #4 flat and pulling medium green c-strokes on half the leaf at a time.
3. On a few of the uppermost leaves, dry brush mint julep to emphasize the highlights.
4. With mint julep, pull a few thin center vein lines on leaves.
5. Sideload dark green and shade down the center of each leaf. Also shade where a leaf passes under a flower or another leaf.
6. Repeat the shading with a small amount of black green – but not in as wide an area as you did with dark green.

Flowers:

Double load a #12 flat brush with one of the color combinations listed below. Place one edge of the brush at the flower center as a pivot point while you pull and wiggle the brush to form the petal. Paint five overlapping petals for each flower, using these colors:

  White/dioxazine purple
  White/true blue
  True blue/lavender
  Dioxazine purple/lavender

• For some flowers, you will have the light color on the outside; for others, the light color is inside. Generally, follow the "white in" or "white out" scheme for each flower grouping.
• When a flower touches the cut edge of the gourd, paint the cut edge with the flower color(s).

Flower Centers:

1. Paint the center of each flower with black. Pull streaks of black out a short distance on the biggest petal.
2. With primary yellow, paint a comma stroke on each side of the black center.
3. Dab a touch of pumpkin where the yellow comma strokes meet.

Accents & Shadows:

1. Add touches of blues and purples on a few leaves along the edge, diluting the paint with water or glazing medium so the colors are transparent.
2. Use a sideloaded brush with burnt umber to shade under the edges of the leaves and under the flowers on the basketweave. Add a few touches of the transparent blues and purples in these shadow areas. Let dry.

FINISH

Varnish or apply wax. ❏

Pansy Purse Patterns

Enlarge @165% for actual size.

See page 50 for instructions.

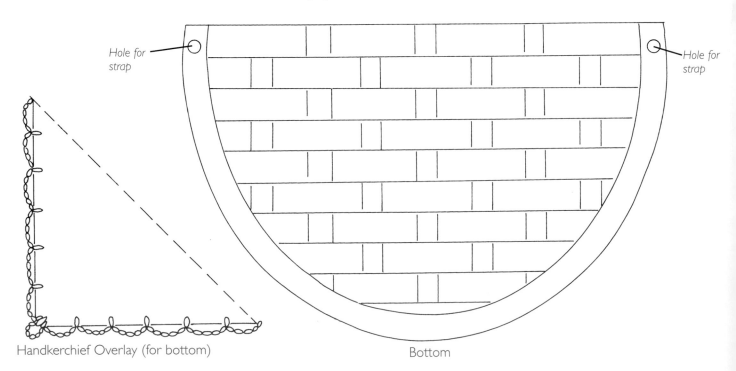

Hole for strap

Hole for strap

Handkerchief Overlay (for bottom)

Bottom

Pansy Purse Pattern
(actual size)

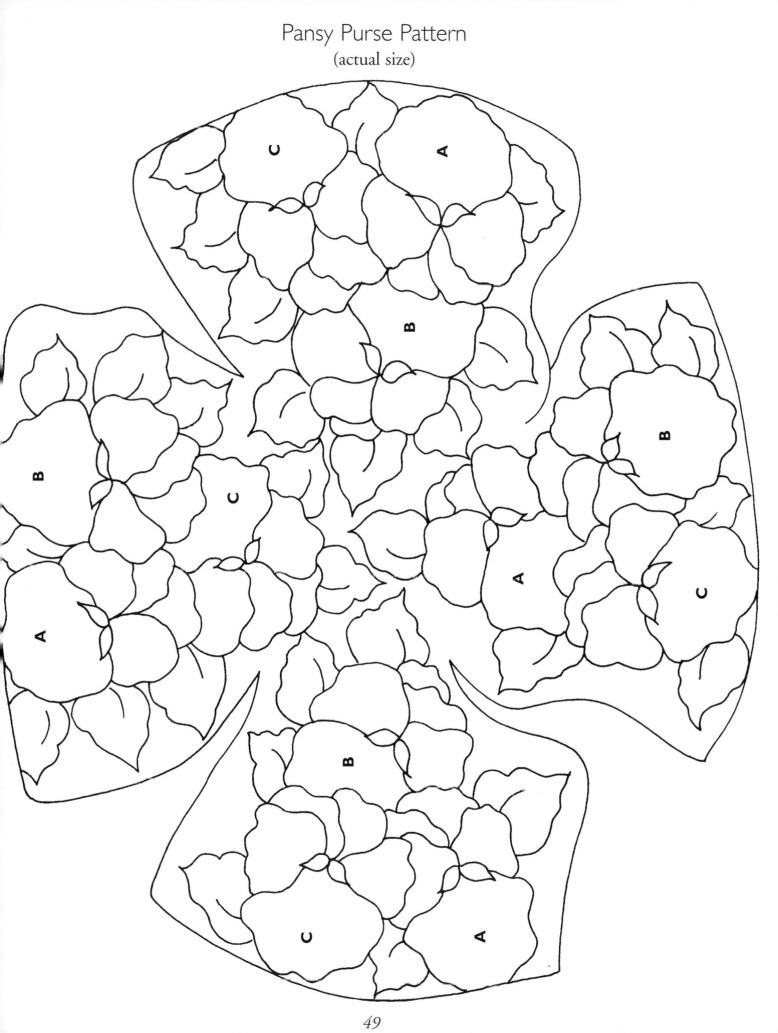

PANSY PURSE
DECORATIVE PAINTED

By Laraine Short

Pattern appears on page 48.

SUPPLIES

Decorating Materials:

Canteen gourd, approximately 7" in diameter

Acrylic craft paint:
Boysenberry
Cadmium orange
Cadmium yellow
Camel
Cherry red
Cool white
Dioxazine purple
Green mist
Gray sky
Dark green
Lamp black
Lavender
Limeade
Pink chiffon
Raw sienna
Taffy cream
Wisteria

Black cording for strap, 1/4" wide, 48" long

2 hinges, 3/4" x 1"

Brass latch

12 brass screws, size 4-40 x 3/8

12 hex nuts, size 4-40

Exterior clear gloss varnish

Tools & Equipment:

Sea sponge

Drill & drill bits

Cutting and cleaning tools

Screwdriver

Brushes:
Angulars - 1/2", 3/8"
Shader - #16
Filbert - #8
Script liner - 20/0
Grass comb - 3/8"

PREPARE

1. Cut off one third of the gourd, using the photo as a guide. Clean the inside.
2. Drill 1/4" hole on sides of bottom portion of gourd 1/2" from top edge (for strap).
3. Drill 3/32" holes for hinges (on the back) and latch (on the front) in both pieces of gourd.

PAINT

Background:
1. Dampen the sponge. Sponge the upper section of the gourd, inside and outside, with two coats dark green. Let dry.
2. Sponge the lower section of gourd, inside and outside, with two coats camel. Let dry.
3. Transfer the designs for the basket and the pansies (but not the handkerchief).

Basket:
1. Shade with raw sienna.
2. Use a grass comb brush to paint basket-like lines with raw sienna. Highlight with taffy cream. Let dry.

Handkerchief:
1. Transfer pattern.
2. Dilute cool white with water so the paint is transparent. Basecoat hankie.
3. Use a grass comb with thinned cool white to brush the thread lines.
4. Load a liner with cool white and paint the crocheted edging. Shade with gray sky.

Pansies:
On the pattern, the pansies are marked "A," "B," and "C."
1. Basecoat "A" pansies with wisteria. Shade with lavender. Deepen shading with dioxazine purple. Highlight with cool white.
2. Basecoat "B" pansies with taffy cream. Shade with cadmium yellow. Deepen shading with cadmium orange. Highlight with cool white.
3. Basecoat all "C" pansies with pink chiffon. Shade with boysenberry. Deepen shading with cherry red. Highlight with cool white.

Flower Centers:
1. Basecoat with cadmium yellow. Shade with cadmium orange.
2. Thin lamp black with water and paint lines.

Leaves:
Since the background is dark green, you are defining the leaves with floated color.
1. Float edges of leaves with green mist.
2. Paint vein lines with green mist. Let dry.

FINISH

1. Brush on two coats of exterior varnish. Let dry.
2. Screw on hinges and latch.
3. Tie on strap. ❑

JAGUAR PURSE
DECORATIVE PAINTED

By Laraine Short

Pattern appears on page 54.

SUPPLIES

Decorating Materials:

Canteen gourd, 8" diameter

Acrylic craft paint:
Burnt umber
Camel
Cool white
Dark flesh
Honey brown
Lamp black
Light buttermilk
Marigold

Floating medium

8 brass bolts, size 4-40 x 3/8"

Brass clasp

Brass hex nuts, size 4-40

Brass hinge, 3/4" x 1"

Cord for strap, 1/4" wide, 48" long

1/4 yd. animal print fabric (for lining)

Clear varnish

Tools & Equipment:

Cosmetic sponge

White craft glue

Sandpaper

Scissors

Wood filler

Cutting and cleaning tools

Brushes:
Angulars - 1/4", 1/2"
Script liner - 20/0
Stroke brush - 1"

PREPARE

1. Remove stem and slice gourd in half horizontally. Clean inside.
2. If needed, fill area where stem was with wood filler. Let dry. Sand smooth.
3. Drill 3/32" holes for hinge and clasp.
4. Drill 1/4" holes on front and back halves, located 2-1/4" from each side of clasp. Wipe away dust.
5. Sponge gourd with two coats of lamp black. Let dry.
6. Transfer the outer edge of the jaguar.

PAINT THE DESIGN

1. Basecoat the jaguar with camel, using a 1" brush. Let dry.
2. Transfer details except spots, whiskers, and chin and ear hair.
3. Basecoat nose with dark flesh. Shade with lamp black, using a 1/4" angular brush.
4. Paint eyes with burnt umber and shade with lamp black, using a 1/4" angular brush.
5. Paint irises with honey brown. Shade under lids with burnt umber and shade sides of irises with lamp black, using a 1/4" angular brush.

Continued on page 54

Pictured above: Inside the purse.

Continued from page 52

6. Float center of each iris with marigold, using a 1/4" angular brush.
7. Paint pupils with lamp black, using a 20/0 script liner.
8. Float around pupil with lamp black, using a 1/4" angular brush.
9. Thin lamp black with water and paint lines coming out of pupil, using a 20/0 script liner.
10. Thin marigold with water and paint lines on each iris, using the script liner.
11. Shade ears with honey brown, deepen shading with burnt umber, and highlight with light buttermilk, using a 1/2" Angular brush.
12. Thin burnt umber with water and paint ear hairs. Repeat with light buttermilk, using a 20/0 Script Liner.
13. Highlight chin with light buttermilk. Repeat twice. Shade with lamp black, using a 1/4" angular brush.
14. Thin light buttermilk with water and paint chin hairs, using a 20/0 script liner.
15. Shade head, sides of nose, and around eyes and cheeks with honey brown. Deepen shading with burnt umber, using a 1/2" angular brush.
16. Highlight cheeks and lower face with light buttermilk. Repeat two more times, using a 1/2" angular brush.
17. Thin lamp black with water and float under nose. Float above nose with light buttermilk. Use a 1/2" angular brush. Let dry.
18. Transfer whiskers. Thin burnt umber with water and paint dots. Thin light buttermilk with water and paint whiskers, using a 20/0 script liner.
19. Wet surface with water and paint spots with burnt umber, using a 1/4" angular brush. Let dry.

FINISH

1. Attach hinge and clasp. Attach cord.
2. Apply two coats of varnish. Let dry.
3. Cut gusset from fabric according to pattern. See page 52 for instructions. Glue in place.
4. Cut remaining fabric into 1-1/2" squares. Glue to inside of gourd. ❏

Jaguar Purse Pattern
(actual size)

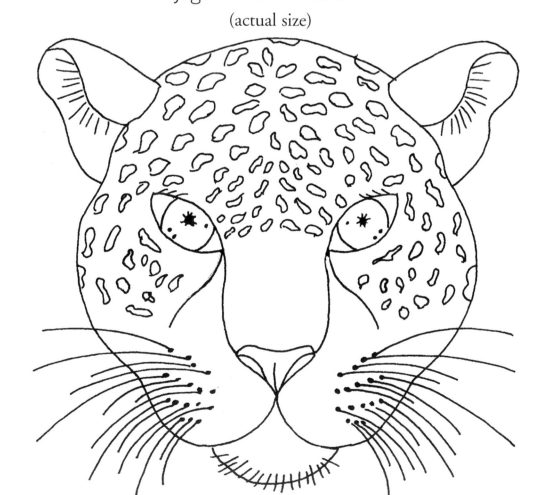

Lining a Gourd Purse

When you make a gourd purse that opens from the top, you need to include a gusset cut from the lining fabric so that when the purse is opened, whatever is in it can't fall out. Here's how to make the gusset.

1. Cut a piece of fabric 24" x 3-1/2". Mark center as shown.

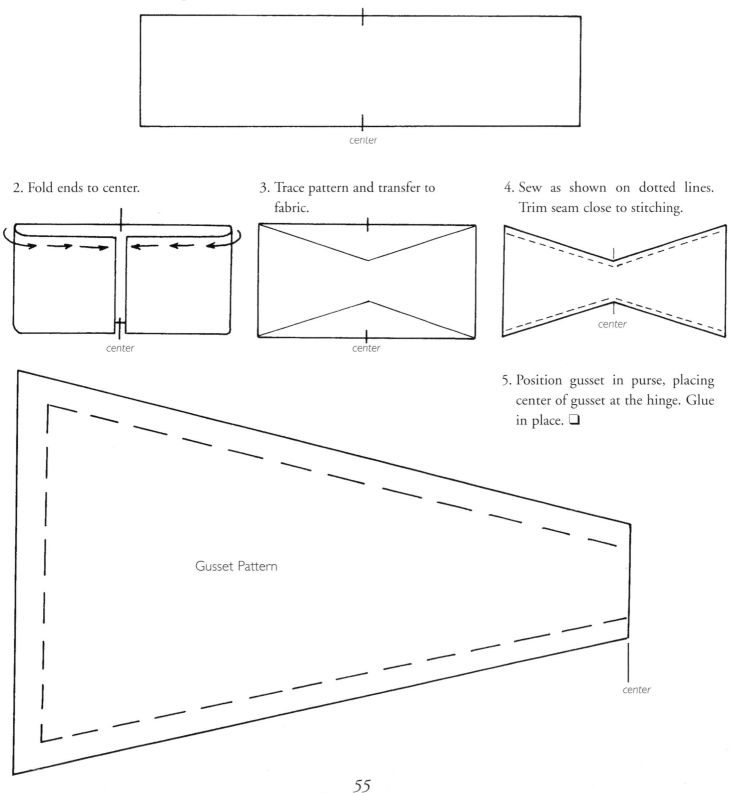

center

2. Fold ends to center.

center

3. Trace pattern and transfer to fabric.

center

4. Sew as shown on dotted lines. Trim seam close to stitching.

center

5. Position gusset in purse, placing center of gusset at the hinge. Glue in place. ❏

Gusset Pattern

center

Magnolia Purse
Decorative Painted

By Laraine Short

Pattern appears on page 58.

Supplies

Decorating Materials:

Canteen gourd, 7" diameter, with a stem

Acrylic craft paint:
Baby pink
Burnt umber
Camel
Cool white
Dove gray
Flesh tone
Green mist
Dark green
Jade green
Limeade
Sable brown

1 brass ring, 5/8"

8 brass bolts, size 4-40 x 3/8"

8 hex nuts, size 4-40

Cord for strap, 1/4" wide, 48" long

Varnish

Floating medium

Glazing medium

Gold metallic elastic cord, 3"

2 hinges, 3/4" x 1"

Tools & Equipment:

Cosmetic sponge

Scissors

Sea sponge

Drill and drill bits - 1/4", 3/32"

Cutting and cleaning tools

Brushes:
Angulars - 1/4", 1/2"
Script liner - 20/0
Filberts - #4, #8
Stroke - 1"

Prepare

1. Cut off a third of the gourd, using the photo as a guide. Leave the stem 3/4" long. Clean the inside.
2. Drill a 1/4" hole on each side of the bottom part of gourd, 1/2" from top edge, for the strap.
3. Drill 3/32" holes for the hinges and another 3/32" one to attach the gold elastic. Wipe away dust.

Paint

Background:
1. With cosmetic sponge, sponge gourd inside and out with two coats dark green. Let dry.
2. Mix glazing medium and green mist. With sea sponge, sponge gourd lightly with glazing mixture. Let dry.
3. Transfer design.

Magnolia & Bud:
1. Basecoat with cool white, using a #8 filbert.
2. Shade with dove gray, then gray mist, using a 1/2" angular brush.
3. Float baby pink under each turned petal, using a 1/4" angular brush.

Magnolia Center:
1. Basecoat with sable brown, using a #4 filbert.
2. Shade with burnt umber and highlight with camel, using a 1/4" angular brush.

Leaves:
1. Basecoat with jade green, using a #8 filbert.
2. Shade with dark green and highlight with limeade, using a 1/2" angular brush.
3. Paint vein lines with limeade, using a 20/0 script liner.

Branches:
1. Basecoat with sable brown, using a #4 filbert.
2. Shade with burnt umber and highlight with flesh tone, using a 1/4" angular brush. Let dry.

Finish

1. Brush on two coats of varnish. Let dry.
2. Install hinges.
3. Loop elastic over ring. Thread end of elastic through hole and knot to secure. Hook loop over stem for closure.
4. Attach strap. ❑

Magnolia Purse Pattern

(actual size)

See page 56 for instructions.

Strawberry Purse Pattern
(actual size)
See page 61 for instructions.

Top

For pattern for bottom, use
the pattern for the Pansy
Purse Bottom on page 48.

STRAWBERRY PURSE
DECORATIVE PAINTED

By Laraine Short

Pattern appears on page 59.

SUPPLIES

Decorating Materials:

Canteen gourd, 7" diameter, with stem

Acrylic craft paint:
  Black plum
  Cadmium orange
  Camel
  Cool white
  Dark green
  Deep burgundy
  Golden straw
  Primary red
  Raw sienna
  Taffy cream

Cord for strap, 1/4" wide, 48" long

2 hinges, 3/4" x 1"

5/8" brass ring

8 brass screws, size 4-40 x 3/8"

8 hex nuts, size 4-40

3" gold metallic elastic

Exterior clear gloss varnish

Tools & Equipment:

Sea sponge

Drill and drill bits, 1/4", 3/32"

Cutting and cleaning tools

Brushes:
  Angulars - 1/2", 3/8"
  Shader - #16
  Filbert - #8
  Script liner - 20/0
  Grass comb - 3/8"

PREPARE

1. Cut off one third of gourd, using photo as a guide. Clean the inside. Cut the stem to 3/4".
2. Drill a 1/4" hole on each side of the bottom part of gourd, 1/2" from top edge, for the strap.
3. Drill 3/32" holes for the hinges and another 3/32" one to attach the gold elastic. Wipe away dust.

PAINT

Background:
1. Sponge the smaller section of the gourd, inside and outside, with two coats dark green. Let dry.
2. Sponge the larger section of gourd, inside and outside, with two coats camel. Let dry.
3. Transfer designs for basket and strawberries.

Basket:
1. To create the basket, shade with raw sienna.
2. Use a grass comb brush to paint basket-like lines with raw sienna. Highlight with taffy cream.

Strawberries:
1. Basecoat with golden straw.
2. Float with cadmium orange, then primary red, then deep burgundy.
3. Deepen float under leaves with black plum.
4. Make a wash with deep burgundy. Paint squares for seed pockets.
5. Paint seeds with dark green. Highlight with golden straw.
6. Dry brush cool white to highlight, making honeycomb shapes in the center of the strawberry.

Leaves:
The background is already dark green.
1. Float edges of leaves with green mist.
2. Paint vein lines with green mist. Let dry.

FINISH

1. Brush on two coats of exterior varnish. Let dry.
2. Install hinges.
3. Loop elastic over ring. Thread end of elastic through hole and knot to secure. Hook loop over stem for closure.
4. Attach strap. ❏

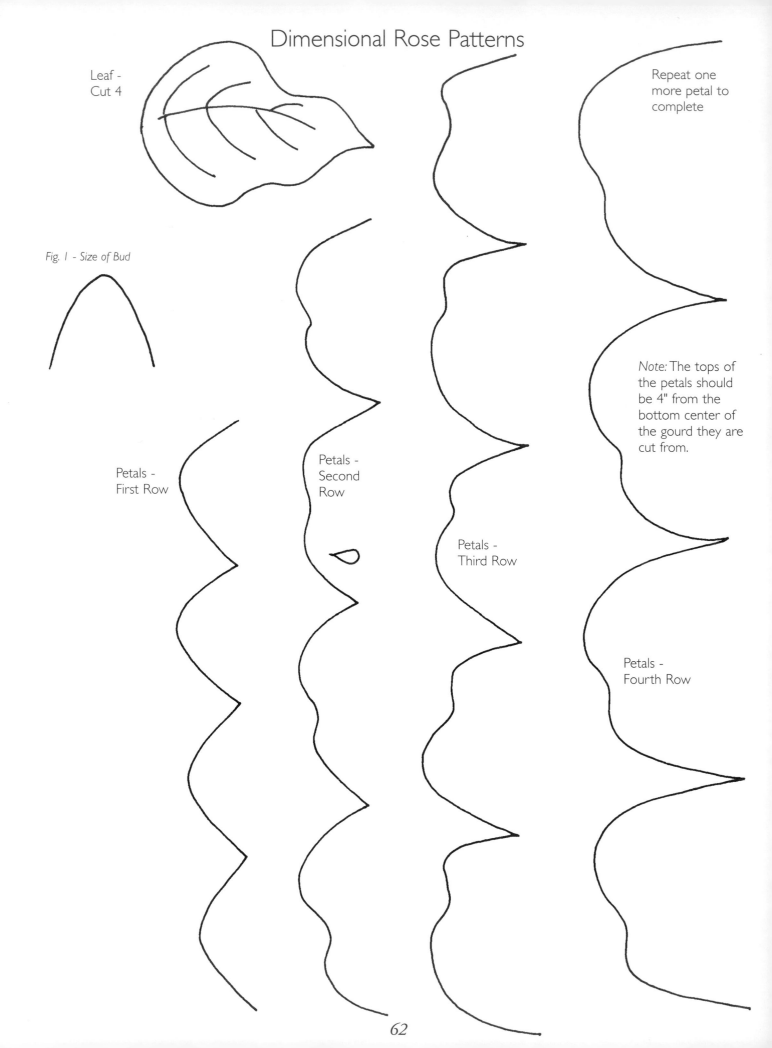

Dimensional Rose Patterns

Leaf -
Cut 4

Repeat one
more petal to
complete

Fig. 1 - Size of Bud

Note: The tops of
the petals should
be 4" from the
bottom center of
the gourd they are
cut from.

Petals -
First Row

Petals -
Second
Row

Petals -
Third Row

Petals -
Fourth Row

DIMENSIONAL ROSE SCULPTURE
CUT & PAINTED

By Laraine Short

Finished size: 4" wide, 3" tall. Circumference is 12-3/4".

SUPPLIES

Decorating Materials:

1 banana gourd

4 small kettle gourds in graduated sizes

Gourd pieces to make 4 leaves

Acrylic craft paint:

Black plum	Brilliant red
Cool white	Deep burgundy
Dark green	Jade green
Limeade	

Floating medium

Glue

Varnish

Tools & Equipment:

Scissors

Cutting and cleaning tools

Brushes:
Angulars - 1/4", 1/2"
Script liner - 20/0
Stroke brush - 1"

PREPARE

Clean gourds and let dry.

CUT & GLUE

1. Cut 4 leaves from gourd pieces.
2. Cut a piece from the end of the banana gourd about 2-3/4" long. (It should look like a bud. See Fig. 1.)
3. Using the pattern provided, cut first row of petals from smallest kettle gourd. Make four petals, each about 1-1/2" wide.
4. Using the pattern provided, cut the second row of petals from the next largest kettle gourd. Make four petals, each about 2" wide.
5. Using the pattern provided, cut the third row of petals from the next largest kettle gourd. Make five petals, each about 2" wide.
6. Using the pattern provided, cut the

fourth row of petals from the largest kettle gourd. Cut five petals, each about 2-5/8" wide.

PAINT

Rose:

1. Basecoat petals with deep burgundy, using 1" stroke brush.
2. Highlight with 2 coats brilliant red, using 1/2" angular brush.
3. Transfer water drop to second row.
4. Shade behind water drop with black plum and highlight with cool white, using 1/4" angular brush.
5. Paint reflected light on water drop with cool white, using a 20/0 script liner.

Leaves:

1. Basecoat with jade green. Shade with dark green. Highlight with limeade. Use a 1/2" angular brush.
2. Float tips with deep burgundy, using a 1/4" angular brush.
3. Add water to limeade and paint veins, using a 20/0 script liner. Let dry.

FINISH

1. Brush two coats of varnish on all pieces. Let dry.
2. Assemble, using photo as a guide. Glue. Let dry. ❏

COTTAGE BIRDHOUSE
DECORATIVE PAINTED

The roof of this delightful little birdhouse is made from gourd seeds that were taken from the inside of the gourd when it was cleaned. What a clever idea!

By Laraine Short

Pattern appears on page 66.

SUPPLIES

Decorating Materials:

Bushel gourd, 9" tall

Acrylic craft paint:
　Burnt umber
　Cadmium yellow
　Cool white
　Dark green
　Dove gray
　French gray blue
　Graphite
　Honey brown
　Light buttermilk
　Milk chocolate
　Santa red
　Yellow ochre

Exterior gloss varnish

Raffia

Gourd seeds

Crackle medium

String or wire to hang gourd

Glue – a strong glue such as wood-workers glue is best if you are planning to use this outdoors.

Tools & Equipment:

Cosmetic sponge

Drill & drill bits

Brushes:
　Angulars - 3/8", 1/2"
　Shader - #16
　Script liner - 20/0
　Deerfoot - 3/8"

PREPARE

1. Clean gourd and let dry. Save the seeds.
2. Drill one 1-1/4" hole in center for bird entrance.
3. Drill four 1/8" holes in bottom for drainage and one 1/8" hole on each side to insert hanger.
4. Basecoat gourd with French gray blue to within 3" of stem and to within 3" of bottom of gourd. Let dry.
5. Apply crackle medium according to manufacturer's instructions. Let dry.
6. Brush with light buttermilk. Let dry overnight.

APPLY SHINGLES

The roof shingles are gourd seeds.
1. Starting at the front of the gourd, glue a row of gourd seeds completely around gourd.
2. Second row start in front, and offset seeds from first row. Repeat until top of gourd is covered. Let dry completely.
3. Transfer design.

PAINT

Door:
1. Basecoat with milk chocolate. Shade with burnt umber. Highlight with honey brown.
2. Basecoat handle and hinges with yellow ochre. Highlight with cadmium yellow.

Windows:
1. Basecoat glass areas with yellow ochre. Shade with honey brown.
2. Paint window frames with milk chocolate. Shade with burnt umber.
3. Paint window muntins with milk chocolate.

Steps:
Paint with milk chocolate. Shade with burnt umber.

Vines, Leaves & Shrubs:
1. Dilute dark green with water. Using a liner brush, paint vines around doors and windows.
2. Make stroke leaves, using a brush double loaded with cadmium yellow and dark green.
3. Stipple shrubs, using a deerfoot brush double loaded with cadmium yellow and dark green.
4. Paint flowers with cherry red and cool white.

Stone Walk:
1. Basecoat bottom of gourd with graphite.
2. Float stones with dove gray.

Stem & Shading:
1. Basecoat stem with milk chocolate. Shade with burnt umber.
2. Thin graphite with water and float shading under roof shingles and around door and windows. Let dry.

FINISH

1. Brush on two coats of exterior varnish. Let dry.
2. Insert hanger.
3. Tie raffia around gourd stem. ❑

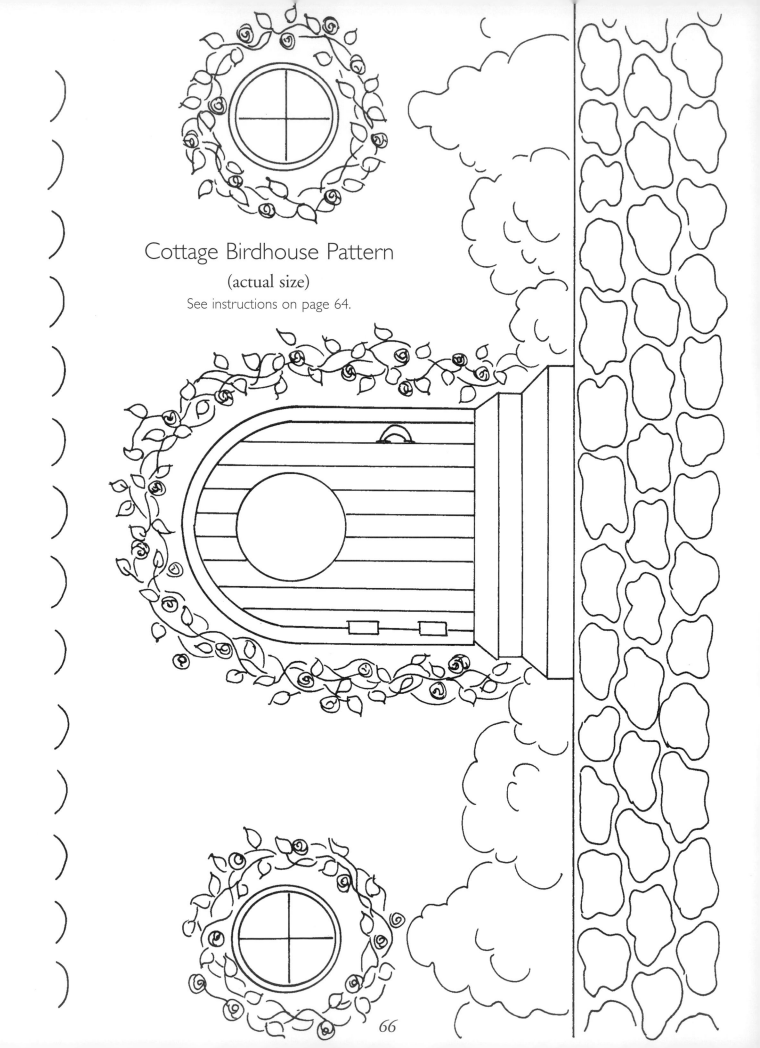

Cottage Birdhouse Pattern

(actual size)

See instructions on page 64.

Blue Porch Birdhouse Pattern

(actual size)

See instructions on page 68.

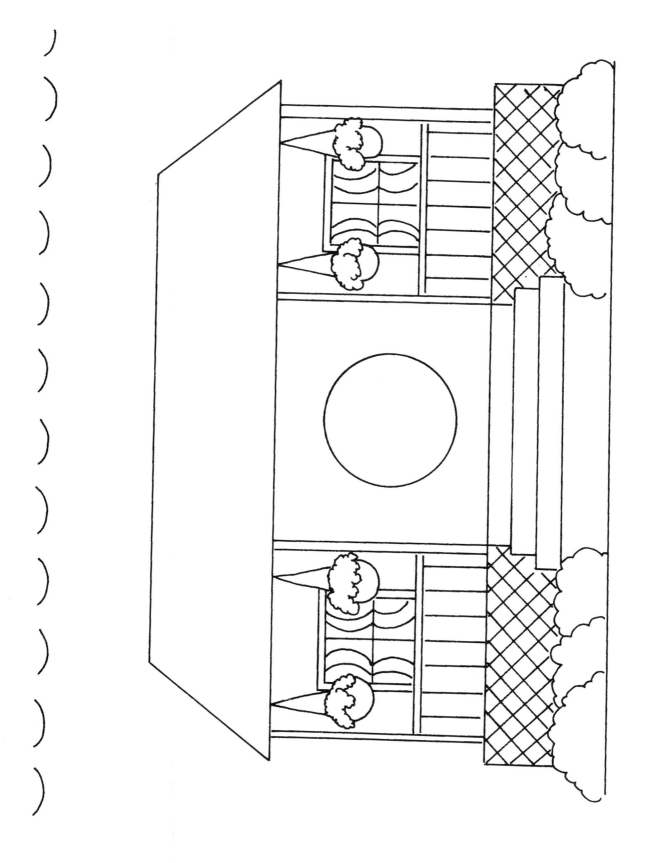

Blue Porch Birdhouse
Decorative Painted

By Laraine Short

Pattern appears on page 67.

Supplies

Decorating Materials:

Kettle gourd, 12" tall

Acrylic craft paint:
  Baby pink
  Cadmium yellow
  Dark green
  Dioxazine purple
  Dove gray
  Honey brown
  Light buttermilk
  Moon yellow
  Orchid
  Santa red
  Slate gray
  Soft black
  Uniform blue
  Winter blue

Exterior clear gloss varnish

Decorative dimensional paste (found in decorative painting supply departments)

String or wire for hanging

Tools & Equipment:

Cosmetic sponge

Drill and drill bits

Chalk pencil

Craft stick

Brushes:
  Angulars - 3/8", 1/2"
  Shader - #16
  Script liner - 20/0
  Deerfoot - 1/4", 3/8"

Prepare

1. Drill one 1-1/4" hole in center for bird entrance.
2. Drill four 1/8" holes in bottom for drainage and one 1/8" hole on each side to insert hanger.
3. Measure 5" down from top of gourd. Mark with a chalk pencil.
4. Dampen sponge and load with light buttermilk. Sponge the paint below the chalk line, applying two coats. Let dry.
5. Transfer design.

Apply the Shingles

1. Use a kraft stick and decorative paste to make shingles on the gourd, starting the first row at the front of the gourd and working around to the back.
2. Start the second row above the first at the front of the gourd, offsetting the placement from the shingles in first row. Finish that row and continue with additional rows until the top of the gourd is covered. Let dry overnight.

Paint

Shingles:
1. Basecoat with uniform blue.
2. Shade with soft black.
3. Highlight with winter blue.

Porch:
1. Basecoat roof, porch, window frames, and railings with uniform blue.
2. Shade with soft black.
3. Highlight with winter blue.

Steps & Windows:
1. Basecoat with slate gray.
2. Shade with soft black.
3. Highlight with dove gray.

Lattice:
Paint with winter blue.

Window Muntins & Curtains:
1. Paint muntins with winter blue.
2. Suggest curtains inside cottage with winter blue.

Plants & Pots:
1. Basecoat hanging flower pots with honey brown. Highlight with moon yellow.
2. Paint pot hangers with soft black.
3. Double load a deerfoot brush with dark green and cadmium yellow and stipple plants.
4. Paint flowers with baby pink and Santa red.

Shrubs:
1. Stipple greenery using a deerfoot brush double loaded with dark green and cadmium yellow.
2. Paint flowers with orchid and dioxazine purple.

Shading:
Thin honey brown with water and float shading under roof shingles and around porch and windows. Let dry.

Finish

1. Brush on two or more coats of exterior varnish. Let dry.
2. Insert hanger. ❑

LEAFY GEOMETRIC CLOCK
WOODBURNED & STAINED

By Betty Valle

SUPPLIES

Decorating Materials:

Penguin or kettle gourd

Wood stain - walnut

Spray paint - brown

Battery operated clock quartz movement with 3/4" shaft

Adjustable hanger with push-in prongs

Clear wax-type shoe polish

Clear satin spray varnish

Tools & Equipment:

Cutting tools, hand and power

Sandpaper

Pencil and paper

Compass

Woodburner with fine tip

Electric drill with 5/16" drill bit

PREPARE

1. Draw a vertical line around the gourd. (Fig. 1)
2. Insert craft knife into line to make a slit. Insert the blade of the power saw in the gourd and cut gourd in half. Set aside one half for another use.
3. Scrape away seeds and pulp from inside of gourd. Sand inside surface smooth.
4. Turn gourd so narrow end is at the bottom. Draw a vertical line. (Fig. 2) At the widest part of the gourd, draw a horizontal line that intersects the vertical line. (Fig. 2)
5. Insert point of compass at intersection and draw a 3" circle (1-1/2" radius). Draw a 4-1/2" circle (2-1/4" radius) around the 3" one. (Fig. 2) This is the clock face.
6. Using an electric drill, drill a hole in the center of the clock face to accommodate the clock shaft.
7. Trace leaf pattern and cut out. Position pattern on the gourd, using project photo as a guide, and transfer leaf shapes to the top and bottom of the gourd.
8. Draw loops in the space between the two circles and numbers 1/2" tall on the face of the clock.
9. *Option:* Add a 1/4" border around the edge of the gourd. Fill in with Xs for a crosshatch design. (Fig. 3)

BURN, STAIN & PAINT

1. Burn the marked designs in surface with fine point woodburner.
2. Fill in the spaces around the leaves and the clock face with squiggles, using the woodburner.
3. Stain the squiggle area of the clock. **Do not** stain the leaves or the face of the clock. Let dry.
4. Spray face of gourd with clear satin varnish. Let dry.
5. Spray inside of gourd with brown spray paint. Let dry. Remove, immediately, any paint that may have gotten on the outside edge.

FINISH

1. Spray several more coats of varnish on the front of the clock. Let dry.
2. Wax surface with clear shoe polish. Wait five minutes and buff with soft cloth.
3. Attach adjustable hanger to back top edge of clock. *Note:* Gourd must be at least 1/4" thick to accommodate hanger.
4. Insert battery in clock works. ❑

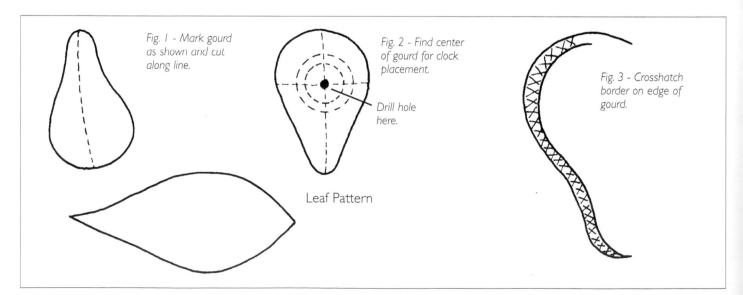

Fig. 1 - Mark gourd as shown and cut along line.

Fig. 2 - Find center of gourd for clock placement.

Drill hole here.

Leaf Pattern

Fig. 3 - Crosshatch border on edge of gourd.

EAGLE & SHIELD
WOODBURNED GOURD

By Betty Auth

Eagle & Shield Patterns

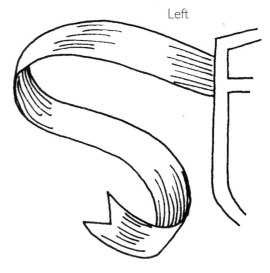

Upper

Right

Left

USA

SUPPLIES

Decorating Materials:

Medium round kettle gourd, 7 to 8" diameter, 9" high

Waterbase satin or matte varnish

Tools & Equipment:

Cleaning and cutting tools

Woodburning tool

Paintbrush - 3/4" flat

Pencil

PREPARE

1. If the gourd has not been cleaned, clean the outside and allow it to dry.
2. Transfer the eagle resting on top of the flag. Add ribbon around the design, curving up, around and to the stem of the gourd. *Option:* If the patterns do not fit on your gourd, use a #2 pencil to lightly sketch and add to the ribbon.

BURN

1. Woodburn the eagle, flag, and ribbon outlines with the flow point.
2. Add finer details with the mini-flow point.
3. Erase all pencil and graphite marks.

FINISH

Brush two coats of matte or satin varnish over the gourd. Let dry between coats. ❏

WOMAN VOTIVE
CUT & WOODBURNED

By Patty Cox

SUPPLIES

Decorating Materials:

Bottle gourd or round gourd with a 5" round base

Acrylic craft paint - black

Tung oil

4" glass votive

Tea light candle

Tools & Equipment:

Craft knife *or* Dremel tool

Woodburning tool

Plumber's putty

PREPARE

1. Cut away top of gourd at an angle.
2. Transfer face outline to each side of gourd.
3. Cut away one side of gourd along each face line.
4. Clean inside of gourd.
5. Paint inside of gourd black.

BURN

1. Transfer design details to each side of the gourd.
2. Woodburn design.

FINISH

1. Place the glass votive in the center of the gourd. Secure with plumber's putty. Place the tea light in the votive.
2. Brush tung oil on outside of gourd. Wipe away after 10 minutes. Allow to cure. ❏

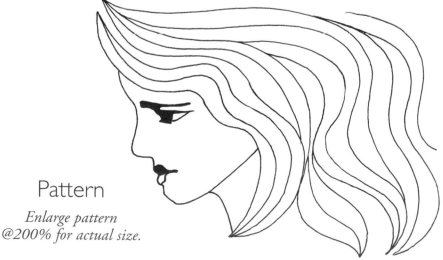

Pattern

Enlarge pattern
@200% for actual size.

Medallion Basket Patterns

(actual size)

See page 76 for instructions.

Twist Pattern

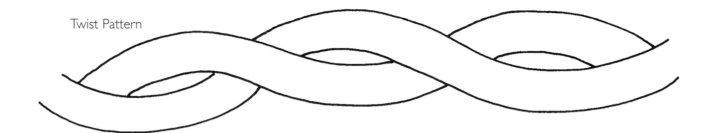

Medallion Pattern

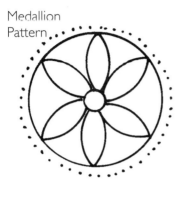

Fig. 1 - Marking the Gourd

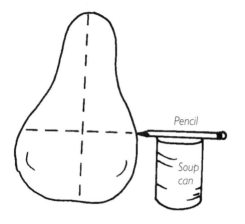

Pencil

Soup can

Fig. 2 - Cutting Out the Basket

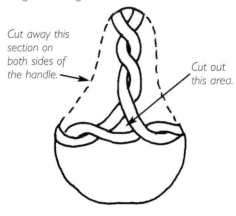

Cut away this section on both sides of the handle.

Cut out this area.

Fig. 3 - Marking the Bowl of the Basket

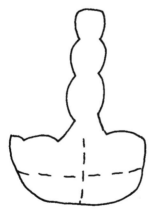

Fig. 4 - Bottom View - Marking Medallion Placement

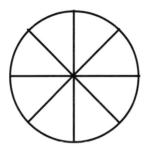

Fig. 5 - Medallion Placement

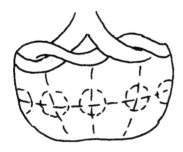

Fig. 6 - Adding the Scalloped Line

MEDALLION BASKET
WOODBURNED & STAINED

By Betty Valle

Patterns appear on page 75.

SUPPLIES

Decorating Materials:

Bottle gourd

Wood stain, walnut and oak

Spray paint - Brown

Clear indoor/outdoor satin varnish

Tools & Equipment:

Cutting tools, hand and power

Cleaning tools

Sandpaper

Pencil

Woodburner with fine tip and shading tip

Soup can

PREPARE

1. Draw a line around the gourd to designate the top edge of the basket. (I used a soup can – see Fig. 1) Cut away stem of gourd.
2. Draw a vertical line around the center of the gourd to determine the placement of the handle. (Fig. 1)
3. Using the pattern provided, draw or transfer the twist design around the top edge of the basket and over the handle. (Fig. 2) All gourds vary in shape, so you may have to adjust the pattern to fit.
4. Cut away the excess gourd on the pencil lines to form the basket.
5. Clean out the seeds and pulp. Sand the interior until it is smooth. Pay close attention to the inside of the handle and the edges.
6. Draw a line around the widest part of the gourd. (This is where the medallions will be placed.) (Fig. 3)
7. Draw lines to divide the bowl of the basket in eight equal sections. (Fig. 4)
8. Trace the medallion pattern and transfer the medallions where the vertical dividing lines and the horizontal lines cross. (Fig. 5)
9. Draw a scalloped line around the gourd beneath the medallions. (Fig. 6)

BURN & STAIN

1. Burn the design on the gourd, using the fine tip of the woodburner.
2. Fill in dark areas of the medallions with the shader tip.
3. Use the fine point of the woodburner to make small dots abound the medallions and the scallop.
4. Burn in your signature and the date on the bottom of the gourd.
5. Stain the gourd. I used two different shades – walnut for the bottom and handle and oak for the center section around the medallions. I did not apply any color to the daisy motifs in the medallions.
6. Spray the outside of the gourd with one light spray of satin varnish. Let dry.
7. Spray inside of gourd with brown spray paint. Let dry. Immediately wipe away any paint that may have gotten on the outside.

FINISH

Apply three more light coats of satin varnish to the outside and one coat to the inside. ❏

HAPPY BLUEBIRD
PAINTED SCULPTURE

By Patty Cox

Patterns appear on pages 80-81.

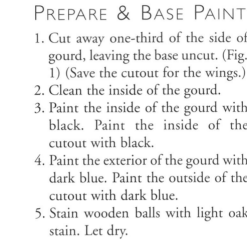

SUPPLIES

Decorating Materials:

Bottle gourd, 12"

Acrylic craft paints - Dark blue, white, black

Polymer clay - Terra cotta

3 wooden doll heads, 1-1/2"

Wood stain - Light oak

Clear acrylic spray finish

Varnish

Tools & Equipment:

Glue (epoxy-type or E6000)

Craft knife

Paint brushes - Flat, liner

Toothpicks

Cleaning and cutting tools

PREPARE & BASE PAINT

1. Cut away one-third of the side of gourd, leaving the base uncut. (Fig. 1) (Save the cutout for the wings.)
2. Clean the inside of the gourd.
3. Paint the inside of the gourd with black. Paint the inside of the cutout with black.
4. Paint the exterior of the gourd with dark blue. Paint the outside of the cutout with dark blue.
5. Stain wooden balls with light oak stain. Let dry.
6. Glue ball feet on bird base, placing two in the front and one in the back.

ADD CLAY SCULPTURE

1. Roll three 1/8" x 8" "snakes" of polymer clay. Braid the snakes.

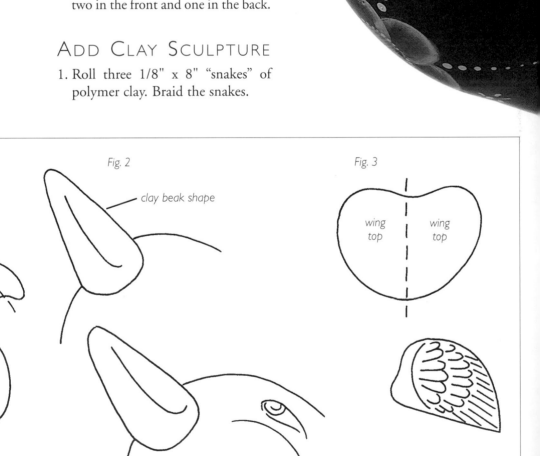

Fig. 1

Fig. 2

clay beak shape

Fig. 3

wing top

wing top

2. Press the braided clay around the top of one wooden ball foot. Form two more clay braids and press at the tops of remaining wooden ball feet.

3. Cut the gourd stem to 1". Form clay over stem in the shape of a beak. (Fig. 2)

4. Bake gourd with clay in a warm oven for 15 minutes (follow instructions on product for oven temperature needed).

Paint

1. Cut the reserved cutout in half to make two wings. Glue each wing on side of bird. (Fig. 3)

2. Trace and transfer patterns. *Option:* Using patterns as a guide, paint designs freehand.

3. Sideload brush with white. Float five petal flowers at head back, chin, base of neck front, at sides under each wing, and at center back.

4. Paint leaves next to flowers at sides, top of head, and base of neck at front.

5. Sideload brush with white. Float a long wavy line on each side of neck.

6. Float an outline around each wing.

7. Using a liner brush, paint scalloped tail feathers, bird wings, eyes, and waved stem at neck back and front.

8. Using paintbrush handle, add dot flowers along stems. Add additional paintbrush handle dots according to pattern. Let dry.

Finish

Spray with a clear acrylic finish. Let dry. ❑

Happy Bluebird Patterns

(actual size)

See page 78 for instructions.

Head and Neck - Top   Head - Side   Neck and Throat - Underside

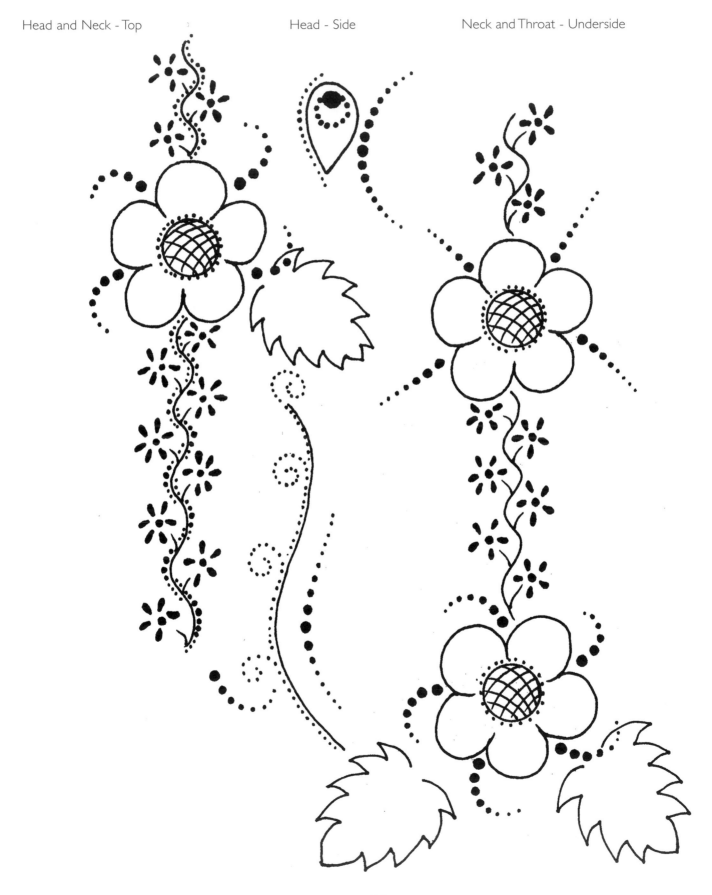

Wing

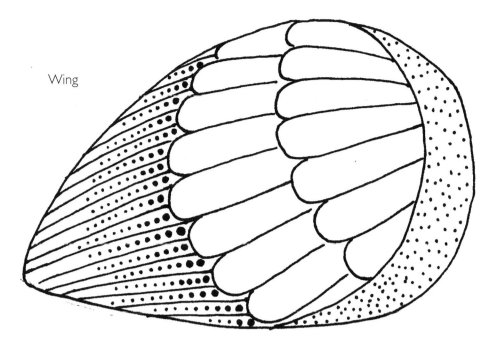

Tail

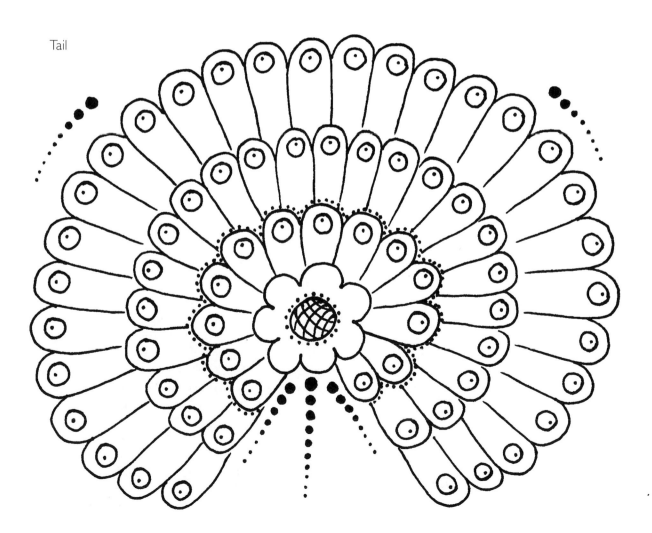

PLANTATION SPRING
PAINTED GOURD

By Aurelia Conway

Patterns appear on pages 85.

SUPPLIES

Decorating Materials:

Martin gourd, 8" diameter

Acrylic craft paint:
  Acorn brown
  Asphaltum
  Barnyard red
  Basil green
  Buttercrunch
  Clay bisque
  Dark gray
  Dark olive green
  Engine red
  Ice white
  Licorice
  Medium green
  Medium gray
  Midnight
  Nutmeg
  Porcelain blue
  Purple
  Sap green
  Titanium white
  Ultramarine blue
  Van Dyke brown
  Yellow light

Waterbase varnish

Wood filler

Finishing wax

Tools & Equipment:

Silk sponge

#000 steel wool

Brushes:
  Brights - #8, #6
  Deerfoot stippler - 1/4"
  Round - #4
  Ultra mini script liner - 20/0

PREPARE

1. Basecoat entire gourd with one coat of clay bisque.
2. Transfer the main elements of design.

PAINT

Sky:

1. Using a large flat brush, apply a wash of porcelain blue to the sky area. Leave about 1/2" of clay bisque showing on the horizon line.
2. At the very top of the sky, near the stem, shade with midnight, walking the color down slightly.
3. At the horizon line, highlight with icy white.
4. Add a few clouds by floating titanium white.

Background Trees:

1. Using a stippler brush with sap green, pounce the background trees. While still damp, highlight using a stippler with basil green.
2. Highlight behind the trees with icy white.

Grass:

Paint the hills and the bottom of the gourd with basil green.

Fence:

1. Paint fence using a liner brush with titanium white. Follow with thin lines of Van Dyke brown.
2. Stipple the foundation foliage along the fence with sap green, followed with highlights of basil green.

Foreground Trees:

1. Base the branches and trunks of the trees with acorn brown.
2. Shade with Van Dyke brown.
3. Stipple trees with dark olive green, followed by basil green while the paint is still wet. Don't lose the darker color – let some branches show through.
4. Stipple foliage at the base of the tree with the same colors used above.

Flower Garden:

1. Stipple the foundation foliage with sap green, followed with highlights of basil green.
2. Base the birdhouse with titanium white.
3. Paint the roof and bird holes with licorice. Shade under the roof with Van Dyke brown.
4. Using a small round brush, dot flowers with these colors, adding a touch of titanium white to each: purple, engine red, ultramarine blue, and yellow light. Use photo as a guide.
5. Add flowers in the same colors along the fence and under the foreground trees, tucked in the green foliage.

Shrubs in Front of House:

1. Stipple the foliage with sap green, followed with highlights of basil green.
2. On the two azalea bushes in the front, add flowers with dabs of engine red + a touch of titanium white.

Clematis Vine (at Chimney):

1. Using a liner brush, paint vines and leaves with sap green.
2. Dot flowers with ultramarine blue + a touch of titanium white.

Magnolia Trees:

1. Paint the branches and trunks with acorn brown. Shade with Van Dyke brown.
2. Stipple the background foliage with dark olive green.
3. While still damp, paint leaves with medium green.
4. Paint blossoms, making four-dot clusters of titanium white.
5. Using a silk sponge, apply medium green to the grass. Use the clean wet back side of the sponge to subdue the color.

Continued on page 84

continued from page 82

6. Shade behind the hills with dark olive green.
7. Highlight the tops of the hills with basil green.

Field:
1. Using the deerfoot stippler, pounce buttercrunch in horizontal rows.
2. Shade the rows with dark olive green. Shade above them with Van Dyke brown.

Trees in the Hills:
1. Using a stippler with sap green, pounce the trees.
2. While still damp, highlight using a stippler with basil green.

Paths:
1. Basecoat with clay bisque.

2. Wash over the paths with asphaltum.
3. Shade one side of each path with Van Dyke brown (keep it light).
4. Shade along the grass edges of the paths with dark olive green.

House:
1. Basecoat with two coats of titanium white.
2. Transfer the details.
3. Paint the roof with licorice.
4. With watered down midnight, base each window.
5. Paint the window trim with titanium white.
6. Paint the shutters and the trim around the door with licorice.
7. Base the chimney with acorn brown. Highlight with clay bisque. Shade with Van Dyke brown.

8. Shade behind the right side of each pillar with dark gray. Shade behind the left side with Van Dyke brown.
9. Shade the other details on the house and door with dark gray.

Barn:
1. Base with Barnyard Red. Indicate the boards with floats of Van Dyke brown.
2. Base in the door with nutmeg. Shade the inner edge with Van Dyke brown.
3. Base the ventilation slats on the side with watered down Van Dyke brown. Let dry. Shade with licorice.
4. Paint the roof with licorice. Trim the windows and edges with titanium white.

Rock Wall:
1. Wash over the wall area with asphaltum. Let dry.
2. Using a stippler, lay in each stone by pushing (not pouncing) with medium gray. Vary the sizes, stagger the rows, and leave space in between each. Let dry.
3. Shade the bottom of each stone with dark gray. Highlight the top with titanium white.
4. Paint the concrete gate posts with the same colors as the stones.

Wisteria on Wall:
1. Stipple the foliage with sap green. Highlight with basil green. Let dry.
2. Add the wisteria blooms by dotting purple + a touch of titanium white. Paint them in clusters.
3. Shade behind the wisteria, under all trees, and around the house and barn with dark olive green.
4. Stipple additional foliage at the base of the wall with sap green. Highlight with basil green. Let dry.

FINISH
1. Apply varnish. Let dry.
2. Apply wax. Let dry and buff with 000 steel wool. ❏

Pictured at left: Back view of painted gourd.

Patterns

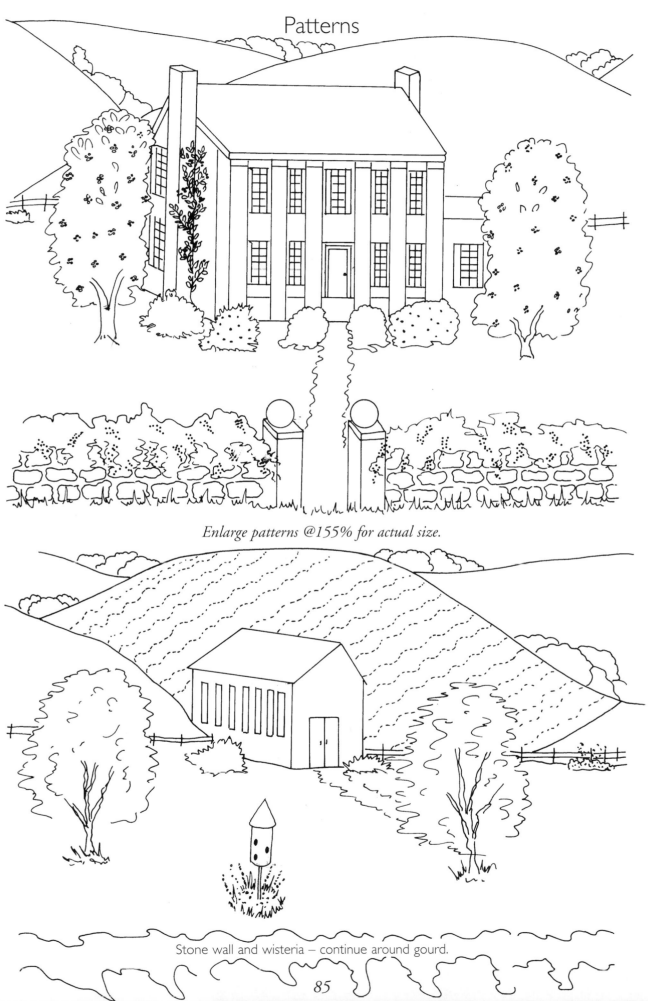

Enlarge patterns @155% for actual size.

Stone wall and wisteria – continue around gourd.

Sunken Tea Garden
Painted Vase

By Aurelia Conway

Patterns appear on pages 89.

Supplies

Decorating Materials:

Martin gourd, 10" diameter

Acrylic craft paint:
Asphaltum
Basil green
Burnt carmine
Clay bisque
Dark gray
Green
Green umber
Ice blue dark
Icy white
Light gray
Lipstick red
Medium green
Medium gray
Midnight
Purple
Sap green
Teddy bear tan
Ultramarine blue
Van Dyke brown
Warm white
Wrought iron
Yellow light

Waterbase varnish

Wood filler

Finishing wax

1/2" cellophane tape

Matte acrylic sealer spray

Tools & Equipment:

2 silk sponges

Cutting and cleaning tools

#000 steel wool

Brushes:
Brights - #8, #6
Deerfoot stippler - 1/4"
Round - #4
Ultra mini script liner - 20/0

Prepare

1. Base paint the entire gourd with clay bisque.
2. Transfer the pavilion designs (one on the front and one on the back). Cut off the top of the gourd.
3. Clean the inside.
4. Using a damp sponge, cover the inside of the gourd with Van Dyke brown. Lap the color over the cut edge.
5. With 1/2" tape, cover the posts, beams, and roofs of the two pavilions.

Paint the Design

Background:

1. Paint the entire gourd with basil green (except, of course, the taped areas).
2. Dampen the silk sponges. With one sponge, cover one area of the gourd with medium green.
3. While still wet, use the other sponge to dab and blend the color. (You want some of the base color to show through.) Continue, working one small area at a time, until done. Let dry.
4. Transfer the bridge, stream, path, statue, and foreground bonsai trees to one side.
5. Repeat the design on the back, reversing the bridge to give the illusion that you are looking through to the other side.
6. Sponge the background trees with wrought iron. Add touches of green while the paint is damp. Don't lose the dark values. Let dry.
7. Shade just under the background trees with wrought iron.

Stream:

1. Base with ice blue dark.
2. Highlight the upper edge with icy white.
3. Shade the bottom edge with midnight.

Bridge:

1. Basecoat with clay bisque.
2. Re-coat with teddy bear tan.
3. Shade the details of the steps with asphaltum.
4. Mix teddy bear tan with a drop of Van Dyke brown. Using a liner brush, add the railing details.
5. Shade under the bridge with Van Dyke brown.

Path:

1. Basecoat with clay bisque.
2. Shade the right side with asphaltum.
3. Shade the grass edges with green umber.

Statue:

1. Base the statue with light gray.
2. Transfer the details. Shade all of the details with dark gray.
3. Base the platform with medium gray. Shade with dark gray.

Bonsai Trees:

1. With a liner brush, base the trunks and branches of the trees with Van Dyke brown.
2. Using the deerfoot stippler, pounce the foliage of the trees with sap green. While wet, add basil green highlights to the tops.

Japanese Maple Trees:

1. Paint the trunks on the grass area with teddy bear tan + a dot of Van Dyke brown. *Note:* You can't see

Continued on page 88

continued from page 86
the trunks of the trees in the background.

2. Using a small stippler or round brush, pounce foliage with burnt carmine and lipstick red. There should be gaps in the leaves so the background shows through.

Lanterns:

1. Paint the bases with lipstick red. Shade the top and right side with burnt carmine.
2. Paint the tops with light gray. Shade the edges with dark gray.

Shrubs & Flower Foliage:

This includes the foliage around the base of the statue, behind the posts, along the stream, and under the trees.

Keep the topiaries in the foreground compact and round.
Using a deerfoot stippler, pounce the foliage with sap green. While wet, add highlights of basil green.

Flowers:

1. Paint the flowers on the bushes by the bridge with purple + a touch of warm white.
2. Using a small round brush, dot the flowers by the stream and under the statues with yellow light, ultramarine blue, or lipstick red, each with a dab of warm white.
3. Paint the flowers under the topiaries with lipstick red + a dab of warm white.

Rocks:

1. Using the deerfoot stippler, dab *(not pounce)* with medium gray. Let dry.
2. Highlight the tops with light gray. Shade the bottoms with Van Dyke brown.

Posts and Beams:

1. Remove the tape carefully.
2. Basecoat the posts with lipstick red.
3. Shade the right sides with burnt carmine. Highlight the left sides with clay bisque.
4. Base the bottom platform and steps with medium gray. Highlight the edge with light gray. Shade with dark gray.
5. Reinforce the bottom edges of the steps with Van Dyke brown.
6. Base the roof with dark gray.
7. Load a #8 bright brush with light gray and medium gray. Blend only slightly. Paint each roof shingle with one brush stroke, staggering the rows as you move upward. (There should be three rows.) Let dry.

Shading:

1. Shade behind the left side and under each shingle with Van Dyke brown.
2. Shade along the top edge of the gourd with Van Dyke brown.
3. Behind the platform base of the pavilion and in front, shade with Van Dyke brown. Use Van Dyke brown to shade under the foreground foliage.
4. Along the edge of the path and stream and behind and under all foliage, shade with green umber. Let dry.

FINISH

1. Seal with varnish. Let dry.
2. Apply wax. Let dry. Buff with 000 steel wool.
3. Spray the inside with matte sealer. ❑

Pictured at left: Side view of painted gourd.

Patterns

Enlarge patterns @135% for actual size.

Side
Fit this design
between the posts
of the pavilion,
matching the trees.

Front and Back
(Reverse on back.)

PAINTED PANDA
PAINTED GOURD

By Susan Ebel

Pattern appears on page 92.

SUPPLIES

Decorating Materials:

Kettle dried gourd

Acrylic craft paint:

Black green   Black
Blue mist   Cadmium orange
Camel   Dark green
Honey brown   Medium green
Neutral gray   White
Yellow green

plus a paint color that is the same tone as the outside of the cleaned gourd

Varnish *or* finishing wax

Tools & Equipment:

Brushes:
Rake
Round - #6
Flat - #4
Scruffy brushes

PREPARE

Transfer the design.

PAINT

Bamboo Leaves:

1. Using a round brush loaded with medium green, paint leaves, pulling up and away from the panda's head.
2. Dip the tip of the round in yellow green. Pull color down from the tips to emphasize the ends.
3. Sideload a small flat brush with dark green and shade the bases of the leaves as they peek out from behind the panda's head.
4. With dark green, add a single vein line to several leaves.

Fur:

The fur is painted using a dry brush technique and finished with a rake or liner brush. Pull the brush in the direction the fur grows. Pandas do not have long hair, so keep these strokes short.

1. Brush neutral gray around the eye, muzzle, under the mouth, and around the outside edge of his head, but not the ears.
2. Add blue mist to your dirty brush and shade the left sides of the same areas.
3. Use camel to add color to the right side of the head, on the nose, and around the muzzle.
4. Wipe your brush, add white, and stroke in the direction the hair grows. Concentrate the color in the center and feather out the edges.
5. Add neutral gray to the edges of the dark spots, the ears, nostrils, the line of the mouth, the eyes, and under the body edges of the arm.
6. Add black to the centers of the areas painted with neutral gray and carry it out towards the white. (The center areas should be totally black.)
7. Refine the fur with a rake brush. Use white to pull strokes down from the bottom of the mouth, downwards on the muzzle, and around the eyes.
8. Add a small amount of neutral gray and camel above the nose in a triangle and soften the edges with white.
9. Use black for the eye areas, the ears, the arm, and the body.
10. With neutral gray, subtly define the separation between the arm and the body.

Eyes:

1. Define the eye with a crescent of honey brown on the left side and a smaller crescent of watery blue mist on the right side.
2. Float clear water on the upper right side of each eyeball. Tip the liner brush in white and touch on the water – when the white paint hits the water it will spread. Be sure the eyes match. (If they don't, paint with black and start again.)

Nose:

1. Paint with black.
2. With neutral gray, shape the nostrils.
3. Add a touch of blue mist on the right side for a dull highlight.

Details:

1. Use the liner and with black stroke to darken the edge of the eye patch, nostrils, split down the muzzle, mouth hole and along his smile line.
2. Add suggestions of hair around the outside edge of the black areas.
3. Using the liner, pull white hairs from the white areas into the black area.
4. Pull hairs over the mouth line to soften.

Bamboo Leaves - Foreground & Finishing:

1. Paint the bamboo leaves that are on top of the panda's paws with medium green, dark green, and yellow green. Paint them the same way you painted the background leaves, but make these more opaque.
2. Touch up background leaves, as needed.
3. Reapply black green to the bases of leaves behind the head.

Lettering - Optional:

1. Transfer the pattern for the Chinese characters that form the panda's name (in English, it's Hua Mei, which is the name of a panda at the San Diego Zoo).
2. Paint with cadmium orange. (It may take several coats for sufficient coverage.)

FINISH

Varnish or wax the gourd. ❑

Painted Panda Pattern

See page 90 for instructions.

Lettering Pattern
(actual size)

Enlarge @125% for actual size.

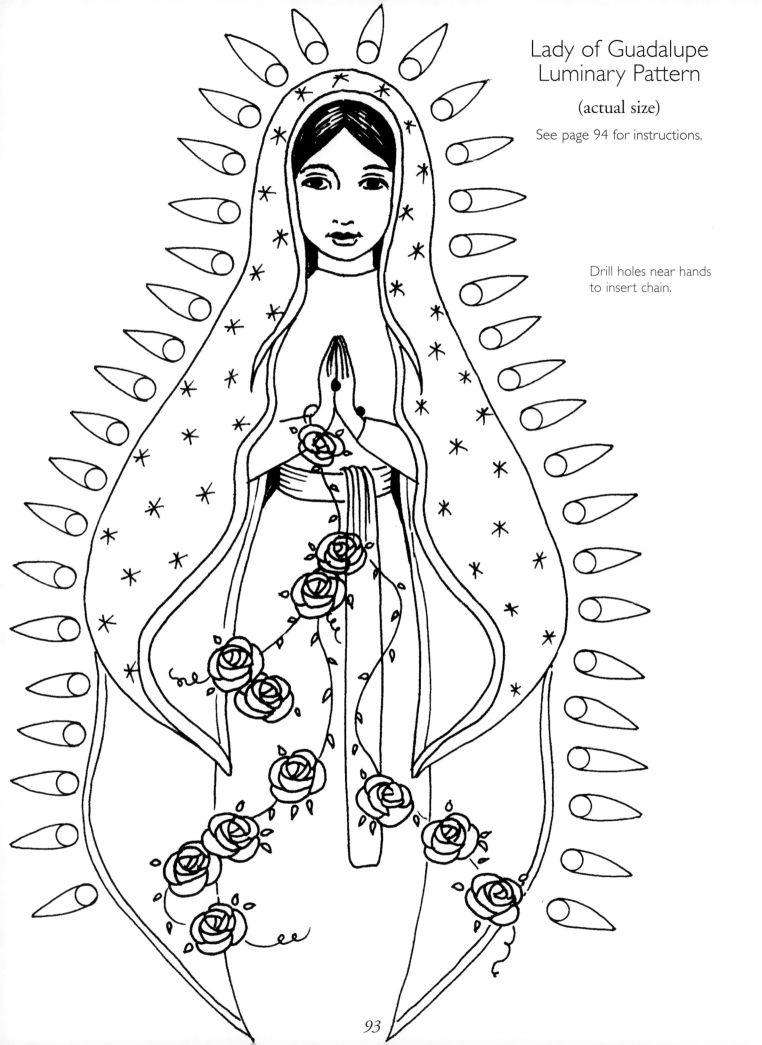

Lady of Guadalupe Luminary Pattern

(actual size)

See page 94 for instructions.

Drill holes near hands to insert chain.

LADY OF GUADALUPE
CUT & PAINTED LUMINARY

By Patty Cox

Pattern appears on page 93.

SUPPLIES

Decorating Materials:

Bottle gourd, 8-1/2" tall

Acrylic craft paint:
    Black
    Dark pink
    Dark blue
    Golden yellow
    Green
    Light gray
    Light pink
    Peach
    Red
    Silver (metallic)
    Tan

Clear acrylic spray finish

Single socket light kit (electrical cord, socket, 5 watt bulb)

4" silver chain

Small silver cross

24 gauge wire

Tools & Equipment:

Craft knife

Paint brushes

Glue (epoxy-type or E6000)

Dremel tool *or* drill

Spring clothespin

Ice pick

PREPARE

1. Cut away one-third of the back of

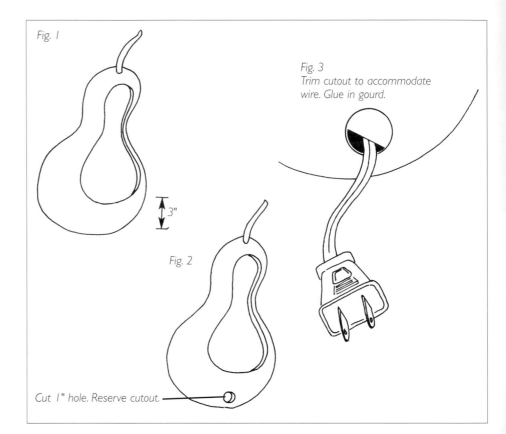

Fig. 1

Fig. 3
Trim cutout to accommodate wire. Glue in gourd.

3"

Fig. 2

Cut 1" hole. Reserve cutout.

gourd, leaving about 3" at base. (Fig. 1)
2. Clean inside of gourd.
3. Paint inside of gourd light gray.
4. Trace pattern and transfer outline of pattern to gourd front.
5. Drill 1/4" holes around outline. Using a craft knife or Dremel tool, cut rays from the holes.
6. Cut a 1" circle at the lower back of gourd to insert electric cord and plug. (Fig. 2) Set aside the 1" cutout.
7. Transfer pattern details.

PAINT

1. Paint background with black.
2. Paint dress with red.
3. Paint cape with dark blue. Trim with golden yellow. Highlight top with a silver wash. Add silver stars.
4. Paint sash golden yellow.
5. Paint roses dark pink and pink with green stems.
6. Paint skin peach shaded with tan. Highlight cheeks with pink. Paint lips pink, shaded with tan.
7. Outline and detail with black.

FINISH

1. Insert light kit plug and cord through the 1" hole from the inside of gourd. Pull plug and cord through hole.

2. Secure socket base inside gourd with glue.

3. Cut a notch from the reserved 1" circle that was cut from the gourd. Glue notched circle over cutout with cord extending through notch. (Fig. 3) Allow glue to dry.

4. Paint the gourd patch black.

5. Trim gourd stem to about 3". Cut a 2" stick from discarded stem. Cut a notch in the center of 2" stick. Glue stick on stem, forming a cross. Hold in place with a spring clothespin until glue dries.

6. Slide cross charm on chain. Poke two small holes through gourd with an ice pick. Secure wire to each end of chain. Insert wire through each hole. Twist wires together on inside of gourd. ❑

Pictured below: Back view of the luminary.

WISDOM KEEPER
PAINTED SCULPTURE

By Patty Cox

SUPPLIES

Decorating Materials:

Top of bottle gourd

Spray paint - Off white suede

Colored pencils

Chalk

Acrylic craft paint - Black

Blue leather, 12" x 24"

Trims - Horsehair, feathers, small piece of fur, turquoise beads, arrowhead charm, fish scale

2 large-head straight pins

Clear acrylic matte finish

2 jumbo craft sticks

Embroidery floss

Tools & Equipment:

28 gauge wire

Craft knife *or* Dremel tool

All-purpose glue

Masking tape

Cutting and cleaning tools

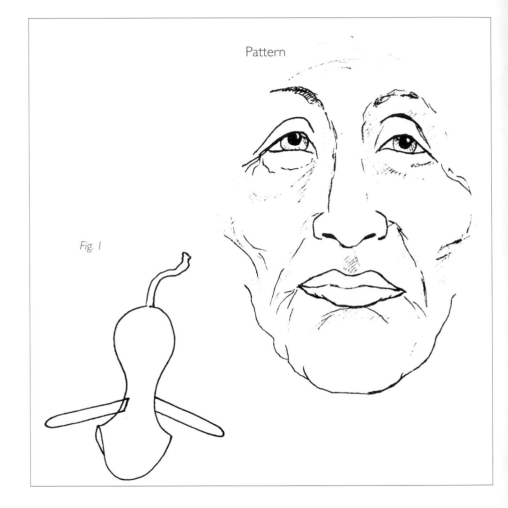

Pattern

Fig. I

PREPARE

1. Cut away top of bottleneck gourd. Clean inside of gourd.
2. Wrap masking tape around gourd stem.

PAINT & COLOR

1. Spray gourd top with off white suede paint. Let dry.
2. Remove tape. Transfer face pattern.
3. Draw face pattern with colored pencils.
4. Shade with chalk and pencils.
5. Spray finished face with matte finish.
6. Paint back of head with black.

DECORATE & FINISH

1. Tie horse hair strands in the center of length with embroidery floss. Tie floss to gourd stem. Glue horse hair strands around head sides, then tie off or tape ends at head back.
2. Paint over hair with glue and water mixture.
3. Wrap and glue strand of turquoise beads at neck. Insert a large-head straight pin through top of arrow-head charm. Insert pin in gourd at bottom center of bead necklace.
4. Wrap fish scale in wire. Insert large head straight pin through wire wrapped fish scale. Insert pin in gourd for earring.
5. Cut slits on each side of gourd. Insert jumbo craft sticks in each slit for shoulders. (Fig. 1)
6. Drape and glue leather over shoulders.
7. Glue feathers and fur at head top. Wrap wire around stem. Form a hanging loop from wire, securing wire to stem. ❏

FRUIT OF THE GOURD
PAINTED APPLE, BANANA, PEPPER

As you work, look at real fruits and vegetables and compare them to your painted gourds. Nature is the best reference.

By Susan Ebel

Apple Gourd

SUPPLIES

Decorating Materials:

Apple gourd

Acrylic craft paint:
  Black plum
  Burnt umber
  Cadmium orange
  Deep burgundy
  True red
  White
  Yellow green

Watercolor paper

Finishing wax

Tools & Equipment:

20 gauge wire

Wire cutters

White craft glue

Drill and drill bit

Mini craft saw *or* craft knife

Cleaning tools

Paint brushes

PREPARE

1. Cut the slice from the gourd, using a mini craft saw or a craft knife. (Fig. 1)
2. Clean the inside of the gourd.
3. Drill holes in the slice and the gourd as indicated.
4. Cut a piece of wire 20" long. Starting at the bottom of the gourd, thread wire through the hole in the gourd and the hole in the bottom of the slice, allowing extra wire between the pieces so the gourd slice can fall open easily. Next, run the wire up to the upper hole in the apple slice and through the hole, keeping the wire taut as shown in Fig. 1. Make a large loop in the top of the wire. (The loop will attach around the stem of the gourd.)
5. Attach the slice to the bottom and top of the gourd.

PAINT THE APPLE

1. Paint the inside of the gourd with watered down white. (You may need several coats.)
2. Place all the colors (except burnt umber) on your palette. Load your brush with true red.
3. Paint the gourd with true red, using brush strokes that follow the contour from the stem to the bottom. Streak with deep burgundy. Let dry.
4. Dry brush black plum to add more depth to the dark areas.

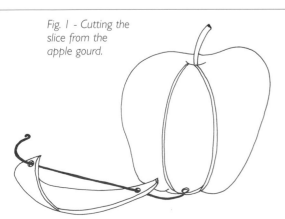

Fig. 1 - Cutting the slice from the apple gourd.

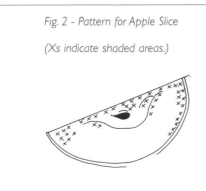

Fig. 2 - Pattern for Apple Slice

(Xs indicate shaded areas.)

5. Add highlights to a few spots at the top and bottom with transparent yellow green. Use a touch of cadmium orange on the side to brighten the entire apple.
6. Spatter the apple lightly with deep burgundy.
7. Separate the gourd slice and paint the cut edges with various red.

CREATE & PAINT THE APPLE SLICE

1. Cut a square of watercolor paper large enough to cover the apple slice. Fold the paper in half and make a sharp crease.
2. Apply white glue to the edges of the apple slice and to the wire running from top to bottom of the slice. Place the watercolor paper over the glue area and hold until the glue starts to set up. Let the glue dry completely before proceeding.
3. Use a craft knife to carefully cut the excess watercolor paper around the apple slice.
4. With true red + a little burnt umber paint the apple skiff – the thin edge around the outside of the slice. (Fig. 2)
5. Sideload with burnt umber, using a lot of water, and shade the edge of the apple and around the core. (Fig. 2) With stronger burnt umber, paint the seed. Let dry.

FINISH

Apply wax to the red-painted surfaces and buff to shine. ❑

Bananas

SUPPLIES

Decorating Materials:

4 to 5 banana-shaped gourds

Acrylic craft paint:
  Burnt umber
  Golden straw
  Light green
  True ochre

Finishing wax

Tools & Equipment:

20 gauge wire
White craft glue

Drill and drill bit
Cleaning tools
Paint brushes

PREPARE

1. Clean gourds.
2. Drill small holes through the top of each gourd to string them together as a bunch after you paint them.

PAINT

1. Load a brush with golden straw and paint the gourds from stem to end. Dip in true ochre occasionally.
2. Sideload with transparent burnt umber and add lines on the peel.
3. Use a little light green on the edges of the peel and at the top.
4. Darken the tops and the ends with burnt umber.
5. Spatter in a few places with watery burnt umber. Let dry.

FINISH

1. Wire the bunch together.
2. Wax and buff. ❑

Green Pepper Gourd

SUPPLIES

Decorating Materials:

Apple gourd (Choose one that is elongated (taller) rather than rounder.)

Acrylic craft paint:
  Dark green
  Medium green
  Pumpkin
  Yellow green

Finishing wax

Tools & Equipment:

Cleaning tools
Paint brushes

PREPARE

Clean the gourd.

PAINT

1. Load a brush with medium green; occasionally dip in dark green and yellow green. Paint the gourd, stroking from the stem to the bottom of the gourd. Concentrate darks at the stem and to emphasize the indentions down the side of the gourd. Paint the stem, too. Let dry.
2. With pumpkin, add a blush of orange on one top bump of the gourd. Let dry.

FINISH

Apply wax and buff to shine. ❑

GRAPE BASKET
CUT & PAINTED

By Susan Ebel

Patterns appear on page 103.

Patterns appear on page 103.

SUPPLIES

Decorating Materials:

Kettle gourd

Acrylic craft paint:

Black green
Black forest green
Burgundy wine
Camel
Cranberry wine
Dioxazine purple
Forest
Lavender
Light buttermilk
Mint julep
Payne's gray
Red violet
Teal
Terra cotta
True blue
White
Winter blue

Varnish *or* finishing wax

Tools & Equipment:

Cleaning tools

Chalk pencil

Mini craft saw

Brushes:

Flats - #12, #8, #6, #4
Liner

PREPARE

Cut:

1. Using Fig. 1 as a guide, mark the basket shape on the gourd with a chalk pencil.
2. Cut gourd to form basket, using a mini craft saw.

Mark the Basketweave Design:

1. Choose the largest brush you can easily use. (I used a #12.) Each row will be the width of your brush.
2. Set the gourd on a flat surface. If it doesn't sit securely, sand the bottom to flatten it.
3. Draw concentric rings, the width of your brush, around your gourd, parallel to the top cut edge of the basket, using a chalk pencil. As you continue up the handle, use the width of a slightly smaller flat brush, such as a #10, to decrease the width of the rows starting about halfway up each handle.
4. To make the vertical guidelines, place a pushpin at the bottom center of the gourd and stretch a rubberband over it and up and over the stem. Loosely draw along the side of the rubber band, move it over, and draw again. (This aids you in achieving the bulging look of the weave.) The width of the weave should loosely correspond to the width of your brush above and below the midpoint. At the "equator," the squares will be wider than your brush. At the "poles," they will be a bit narrower.

PAINT THE BASKET

1. Load your brush with camel and blend on a palette. Sideload with terra cotta and blend again. Paint with the terra cotta edge alternating from the left vertical side to the bottom horizontal side. These colors should blend well with the natural color of the gourd; if the skin color shows, it will only add depth. You may need to reload and repaint some squares. (A streaky look can also be natural. Remain fairly consistent around the gourd so it looks unified.)

Tip: If you like, chalk in the area covered by the grapes and leaves. Don't paint the basketweave underneath those areas.

TRANSFER THE DESIGN

1. Make a template of each of the four grape patterns.
2. Transfer the general outlines of the grape leaves and stems.

PAINT THE DESIGN

Leaves:

1. Base with forest green and paint the cut edge of the gourd wherever it touches a leaf.
2. Highlight the leaves with mint julep in the areas noted with Os on the patterns.
3. Use a thin liner brush with mint julep to paint the veins.
4. Shade the bottom edges of some veins using a small flat brush sideloaded with forest or black forest green. Use black forest green on the darker sides and forest over the highlighted areas.
5. Repeat all the shading with a small amount of black green. Several leaves fold over themselves and the undersides should be very dark.

continued on page 102

continued from page 100

Grapes:

Four color combinations are used for the four bunches of grapes. Paint all the grapes in a cluster with one of the combinations. When a grape touches the cut edge of the gourd, paint the cut edge to match the grape.

1. Transfer the grape shapes.
2. Paint the grapes, using the colors listed below.

    Blue grapes - Base with true blue. Highlight with winter blue. Shade with dioxazine purple and Payne's gray.

    Purple grapes - Base with lavender. Highlight with lavender + white. Shade with dioxazine purple and Payne's gray.

    Red grapes - Base with burgundy. Highlight with burgundy + white. Shade with cranberry wine and Payne's gray.

    Red violet grapes - Base with red violet. Highlight with red violet.

3. Reestablish the highlight on the grape if you have lost it in shading.
4. Add a small shine to the highlight with light buttermilk. On the grapes in the very front of a cluster, touch a tiny dot of white in the middle of the highlight.
5. Paint crescents of reflected light on the lower left of each grape (if that edge is exposed). On the red and the purple grapes, use teal. For the blue and red violet ones, use lavender.

Stems:

1. With burnt umber, lay in the stems. Sideload the right side with camel and light buttermilk to highlight.
2. Mix a bit of dioxazine purple with burnt umber to add sideloaded shadows on the left and bottom edges of the stems.

3. Use a liner brush with burnt umber to add a few curlicues.

Shading & Accents:

1. Use a sideloaded brush with burnt umber to shade under the edges of the leaves and under the grapes.
2. Use the grape colors occasionally to accent the leaves, and add the colors of one grape cluster to neighboring clusters.
3. Wash touches of the grape colors on the shaded area of the basket. Let dry.

FINISH

Varnish or wax. ❏

Fig. 1 - Cutting and Basketweave Guide

Pictured below: Close-up view of grape design.

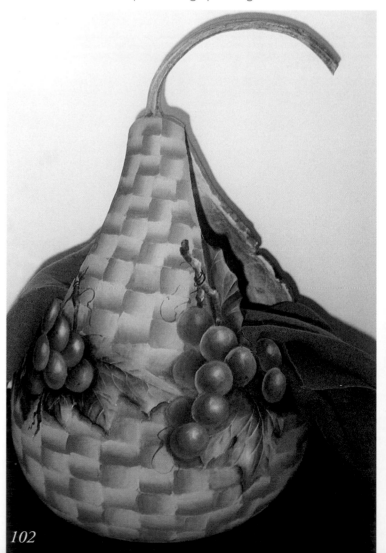

102

Grape Cluster Patterns

Enlarge pattens @200% for actual size.

Purple Grapes

Red Violet Grapes

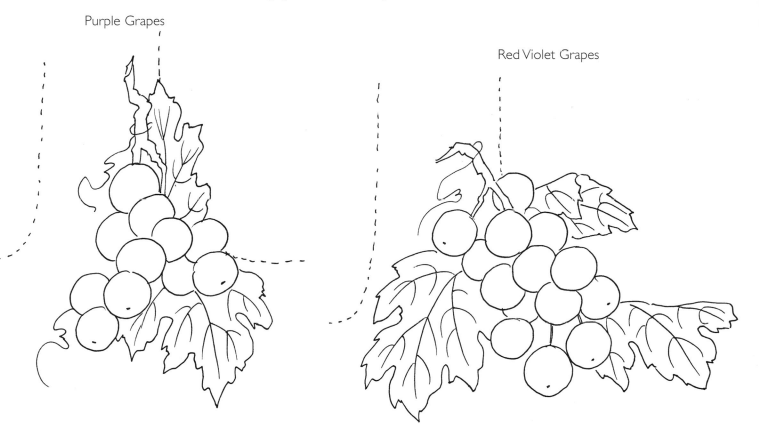

Blue Grapes

Red Grapes

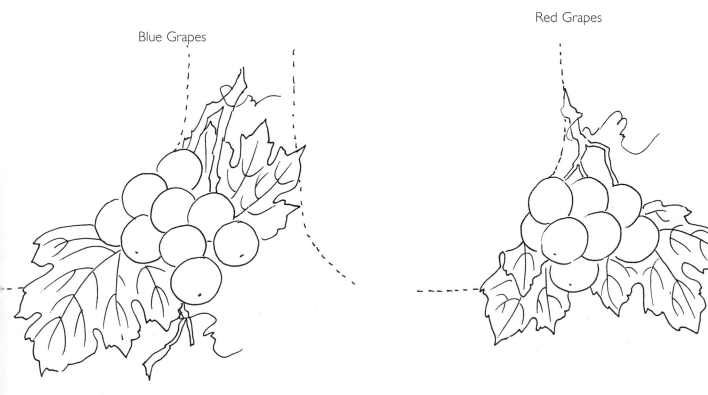

TUMBLING LEAVES
WOODBURNED VESSEL

By Betty Valle

SUPPLIES

Decorating Materials:

Indonesian bottle gourd

Wood stain - Walnut

Oil based colored pencils

Sealer spray

Natural raffia

Tools & Equipment:

Cleaning tools

Cutting tool, hand or power

Wood burner with fine tip

Sandpaper

Pencil and paper

Scissors

Paper towels

PREPARE

1. Draw a line around the narrow part of the neck of the gourd by placing a pencil on something that places the pencil at the desired height for cutting. Place the gourd close to the pencil tip and slowly turn the gourd so the pencil draws a line around the neck of the gourd.
2. Pierce gourd at drawn line with craft knife. Insert saw blade and cut around line *or* use a craft knife to remove top. Set aside the top of the gourd for another use.
3. Using cleaning tools, scrape inside of gourd to remove the excess pulp and seeds. (I find a grapefruit spoon helpful.)
4. Sand the edges of the opening smooth using sandpaper.

STAIN

Wipe stain finish on gourd surface with a paper towel. Wipe off excess with a strong paper towel. Allow stain to dry according to directions of the stain you use.

BURN

1. Trace the leaf pattern on paper. Cut out.
2. Draw a line around the widest part of the gourd using the same method you did for the opening.
3. Position the leaf pattern at random around the pencil line and trace around the pattern. (Perhaps you would like to make a simple cluster of leaves, or maybe you want to cover the entire gourd with leaves – be your own designer.)
4. Burn the leaf design into the surface of the gourd with a fine tip woodburner.

COLOR

Add color to the leaves with oil-based colored pencils.

FINISH

1. Spray over the colored pencil area with a sealer spray. Let dry.
2. Braid three strands of raffia together to form a piece long enough to wrap around the neck of the gourd three times.
3. Apply thick white craft glue around the neck of the gourd and wrap with braided raffia.
4. Tie ends together and loosen braid at ends.
5. If desired, add additional strands of raffia to ends. Wrap a strand of raffia around the whole cluster of loose ends to form tassel. ❏

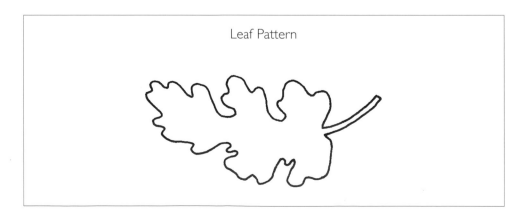

Leaf Pattern

JACK O' LANTERN
PAINTED ORNAMENT TREE

By Laraine Short

Instructions begin on page 108.

Baby Jack O' Lantern

Ghost Jack O' Lantern

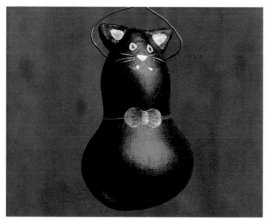

Black Cat

Smiling Witch

Ghost

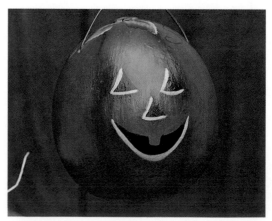

Single-Tooth Jack O' Lantern

Pictured on pages 106-107.

Supplies

Decorating Materials:

Cannonball gourd, 7" x 7"

6 mini gourds in various shapes

Acrylic craft paint:

Antique gold
Blush flesh
Burnt sienna
Cadmium yellow
Cool white
Dark green
Lamp black
Light green
Marigold
Moon yellow
Orange
Santa red
Winter blue

Exterior clear gloss varnish

Raffia

22 gauge wire (for hangers)

Wooden dowel tree (available at crafts stores)

Plaster of Paris

Tin can (fits in hole in top of gourd to hold tree)

Excelsior *or* moss (to go on top of can)

Paperclay *or* air-dry clay

Tools & Equipment:

Cosmetic sponge

Cutting tools

Cleaning tools

Drill and 1/16" drill bit

Brushes:

Angulars - 3/8", 1/2"
Shader - #16
Script liner - 20/0

Prepare

1. Cut a 3" hole in top of kettle gourd.
2. Drill 1/16" holes on sides of mini gourds to hold hangers.

Paint Pumpkins

1. Sponge with antique gold. Let dry.
2. Basecoat with orange. Let dry.
3. Transfer patterns.
4. To give the appearance of pumpkin shape, do back-to-back floats of Santa red where sections of pumpkin would be.
5. Highlight between red sections with back-to-back floats of moon yellow. Let dry.
6. Paint eyes, noses, and mouths with lamp black. Outline with cadmium yellow, using photo as a guide.
7. Double load brush with dark green and cadmium yellow. Paint freehand one stroke leaves.
8. Thin dark green with water. Paint tendrils.

Paint Ghosts

1. Basecoat with two coats cool white. Shade with winter blue. Let dry.
2. Transfer pattern for faces.
3. Thin lamp black with water. Paint eyes, noses, and mouths.
4. Float eyes with winter blue. Add reflected light with cool white.

Paint Witch

1. Basecoat with light green.
2. Transfer pattern.
3. Basecoat hat with lamp black.
4. Paint hat brim with orange. Shade with Santa red. Highlight with moon yellow.
5. Dot eyes with cool white. Add smaller dots of lamp black.
6. Paint brows and mouth with lamp black.
7. Paint nose with Santa red. Float cheeks with Santa red.
8. Paint hair using liner brush. Streak with burnt sienna. Repeat with marigold.

Paint Cat

1. Make ears from paperclay. Let dry.
2. Glue ears in place.
3. Basecoat cat with lamp black. Let dry.
4. Transfer design for bowtie.
5. Paint bowtie with orange. Shade with Santa red. Highlight with cadmium yellow.
6. Paint mouth with Santa red.
7. Paint teeth and whiskers with cool white.
8. Paint eyes with cadmium yellow.
9. Mix Santa red and cool white to make pink. Paint inside ears and nose. Let dry.

Finish

1. Brush two coats of varnish on all pieces. Let dry.
2. Mix plaster of paris and put in can to secure tree. Let dry.
3. Paint wooden tree and can with green.
4. Put can with tree in gourd. Place excelsior around tree.
5. Attach wire to the ornaments. Hang on tree.
6. Tie raffia bow on tree. ❏

Patterns

(actual size)

Autumn Leaves Box
Cut & Painted

By Laraine Short

Patterns appear on page 112

Supplies

Decorating Materials:

Apple gourd, approximately 6" tall, clean and let dry.

Any gourd large enough to cut 6 leaves.

Acrylic craft paint:

Antique gold
Burnt umber
Cadmium yellow
Cadmium red
Cool white
Dark green
Deep burgundy
Honey brown
Jade green
Lamp black
Marigold
Orange

Floating medium

Glue

Varnish

Tools & Equipment:

Palette knife

Pencil and eraser

Scissors

Cosmetic sponge

Cutting and cleaning tools

Brushes:

Angular - 1/2"
Script liner - 20/0
Stroke - 1"

Prepare

1. Cut off top third of apple gourd, using the cut line pictured in Fig. 1 as a guide.
2. Clean gourd and let dry.
3. Using the patterns provided, cut out leaf shapes from gourd pieces. Choose gourd pieces for the leaves that will curve around the apple gourd like the ones in the photo.

Paint

Pumpkin:

1. With cosmetic sponge, completely sponge inside and outside of gourd with antique gold. Let dry.
2. Repeat with orange. Let dry.
3. To give gourd and lid the look of a pumpkin, apply back-to-back floats with cadmium red where pumpkin sections would be. Make six sections, using a 1/2" angular brush.
4. Do back-to-back floats between the sections with cadmium yellow, using a 1/2" angular brush.
5. Basecoat stem with dark green. Highlight with cadmium yellow. Use a 1/2" angular brush.

"A" Leaf:

1. Basecoat with honey brown, using 1" stroke brush. Let dry. Transfer center line.
2. Shade with deep burgundy and highlight with marigold, using 1/2" angular brush.
3. Thin marigold with water and paint veins, using a 20/0 script liner.

"B" Leaves:

1. Basecoat with marigold. Let dry. Transfer center line.
2. Shade with dark green. Repeat with burnt umber. Use a 1/2" angular brush.
3. Thin marigold with water and paint veins, using a 20/0 script liner.

"C" Leaf:

1. Basecoat with jade green. Let dry. Transfer center line.
2. Shade with dark green and highlight with marigold, using a 1/2" angular brush.
3. Thin marigold with water and paint vein, using a 20/0 script liner.

"D" Leaves:

1. Basecoat with cadmium red. Let dry. Transfer center line.
2. Shade with deep burgundy and highlight with marigold, using a 1/2" angular brush.
3. Thin marigold with water and paint veins, using a 20/0 script liner. Let dry.

Finish

1. Place lid on gourd. Position leaves on gourd, using photo as a guide. Glue in place. Let dry.
2. Brush on two coats of varnish. Let dry. ❑

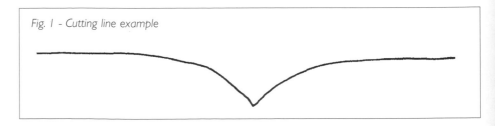

Fig. 1 - Cutting line example

Autumn Leaves Box Patterns

(actual size)

See page 110 for instructions.

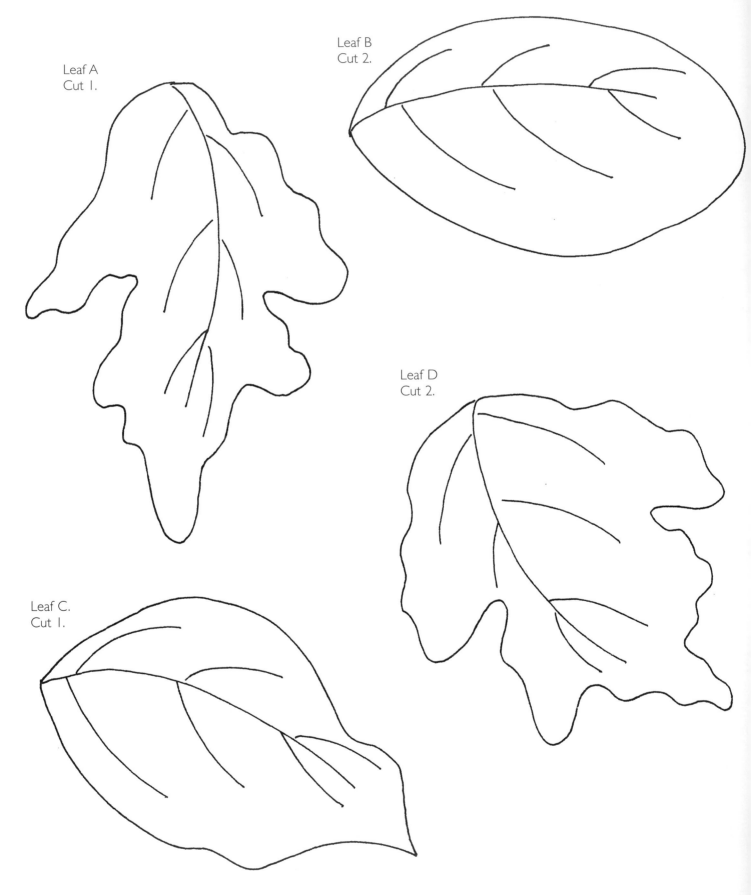

Leaf A
Cut 1.

Leaf B
Cut 2.

Leaf D
Cut 2.

Leaf C.
Cut 1.

Fall Leaves Centerpiece Patterns

(actual size)

See pages 114 for instructions.

FALL LEAVES CENTERPIECE
STAINED & WOODBURNED

By Elinor Tenney

Patterns appear on page 113.

SUPPLIES

Decorating Materials:

Mexican or Chinese bottle gourd

Wood Stains - Blue, golden oak, red, yellow

Gesso

Satin polyurethane varnish

Tools & Equipment:

Sandpaper

Woodburning tool

Craft knife

Hand or electric jigsaw

Metal scrubber or scrub brush

Sea sponge

Brushes:

    Flats - #8, 1/2", 1"
    Basing brush (for gesso)

PREPARE

1. Wash the gourd with a metal brush or scrubber. Let dry.
2. Cut out paper templates for the leaves, using the patterns provided.
3. Find the natural resting position for your gourd and mark the bottom.
4. With the gourd sitting on a flat surface, arrange the leaf templates on the sides of the gourd. Use the photo as a guide and adapt the design to fit your gourd. Butt or overlap the leaves, if necessary.
5. Trace around the leaves with a pencil. (The top of the gourd – above the leaves – will be cut and removed.)
6. Cut with a jigsaw along the tops of the leaves to form the shaped edge. Make some cuts below the edge to create open spaces between the leaves.
7. Clean the inside of the gourd. Scrape and sand the interior.
8. Apply several thick coats of gesso to the interior to create a smooth surface. Let dry.

STAIN & WOODBURN

1. Make these color mixes from the stains:
   Orange mix: 1 part red, 3 parts yellow
   Green mix: 1 part blue, 3 parts yellow
   Dark green mix: 1 part blue, 2 parts yellow
   Brown mix: 1 part green, 2 parts red
   Dark brown mix: 1 part dark green mix, 1 part red
2. Try out the colors on some of the gourd pieces you cut and removed from the top. Adjust mixes as needed to obtain attractive colors.
3. Using your wood burner, burn the edges and veins of all the leaves.
4. Stain each leaf a different fall color, using the color mixes. Add red edges to yellow, green, orange, and brown leaves as shown in the

photo.

5. Stain the bottom part of the gourd with golden oak. Let dry.

6. *Option:* Sideload a flat brush with dark brown stain and shade around the leaves.

FINISH

Apply three coats satin varnish. ❏

CHRISTMAS GOOSE
PAINTED SCULPTURE

By Aurelia Conway

Pattern appears on pages 118-119.

SUPPLIES

Decorating Materials:

Goose gourd, 6" diameter

Acrylic craft paint:

Basil green
Clay bisque
Dark gray
Engine red
Green meadow
Green umber
Licorice
Light gray
Medium gray
Mushroom
Titanium white
Van Dyke brown

Wood filler

Finishing wax

3" square block of wood, 1/2" thick

Wooden dowel, 1/4" diameter, 5" long

Spray sealer

Tools & Equipment:

Silk sponge

Electric drill and 1/4" drill bit

Sandpaper

000 steel wool

Brushes:

Brights - #8, #6
Deerfoot stippler - 1/4"
Round - #4
Ultra mini script liner - 20/0
Filberts - #6, grass rake

PREPARE

1. Sand the wood block. Drill a 1/4" hole in the center. Glue dowel in the center to make the stand.

2. Paint the stand with licorice.
3. Paint the entire gourd with clay bisque. Let dry.
4. Re-coat with titanium white. Let dry.
5. Mark and drill a hole in the center of the bottom of the gourd and insert the dowel, gluing in place. Let dry.
6. Transfer the design (except the wreath).

PAINT

Head & Eye:

1. Base the dark part of the head with licorice.
2. Mark the placement of the eyes. Outline with titanium white.
3. Put highlight dots in the eyes with titanium white.
4. Highlight the line under the eye with medium gray.
5. Shade the inside edge of the white marking on the head with medium gray.

Bill:

1. Base with dark gray. Let dry.
2. Re-coat with a wash of medium gray.
3. Outline the mouth by shading with licorice.
4. Mark the nostrils and base with licorice.
5. Highlight the edge of the bill and under the nostrils with light gray.

Wings & Back:

1. Sponge the white area of the body with light gray, keeping it light. Add hints of medium gray to the bottom area.

Continued on page 118

continued from page 116.

2. Float each row of feathers with medium gray, placing the darker value toward the tail. Make sure there is a space with the lighter value before putting in the next row of feathers. Continue until all rows of feathers are completed.

3. Re-float the feathers a second time with mushroom, walking the color out slightly.

4. Using a filbert rake brush, gently add the hints of feather lines with medium gray. Keep this light and wispy.

5. Shade behind the sections of the wings and back with dark gray.

Tail Feathers:

1. Paint the same way as the wing feathers in the direction of the tail.

2. Shade the edges with dark gray, then darken with Van Dyke brown, especially where the wing overlaps the tail.

Garland & Greenery:

1. Transfer the pattern for the garland to the goose and the pattern for the greenery to the base.

2. Sponge the background with green umber. Let dry.

3. Using a #6 filbert, single stroke the leaves with basil green and a touch of green meadow. Pay attention to the direction of the leaves.

4. Add a few stems with basil green.

5. Using the handle end of a large brush, dot the berries with engine red. Use a brush with a smaller handle to vary the size of the berries.

6. Shade the bottoms of the larger berries with Van Dyke brown. Highlight the tops with clay bisque.

7. Paint the greenery on the base, using the same colors and techniques. Let dry.

FINISH

1. Seal with varnish. Let dry.

2. Apply wax. Let dry. Buff with 000 steel wool. ❏

Christmas Goose Pattern
(actual size)

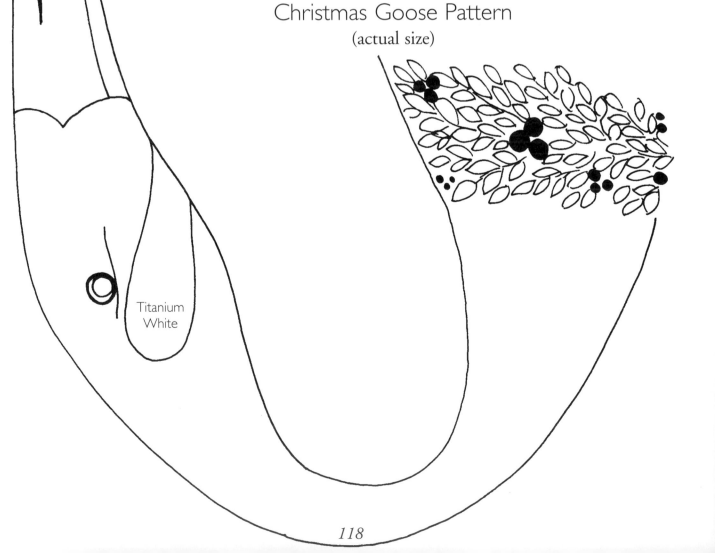

Titanium White

Christmas Goose Pattern

(actual size)

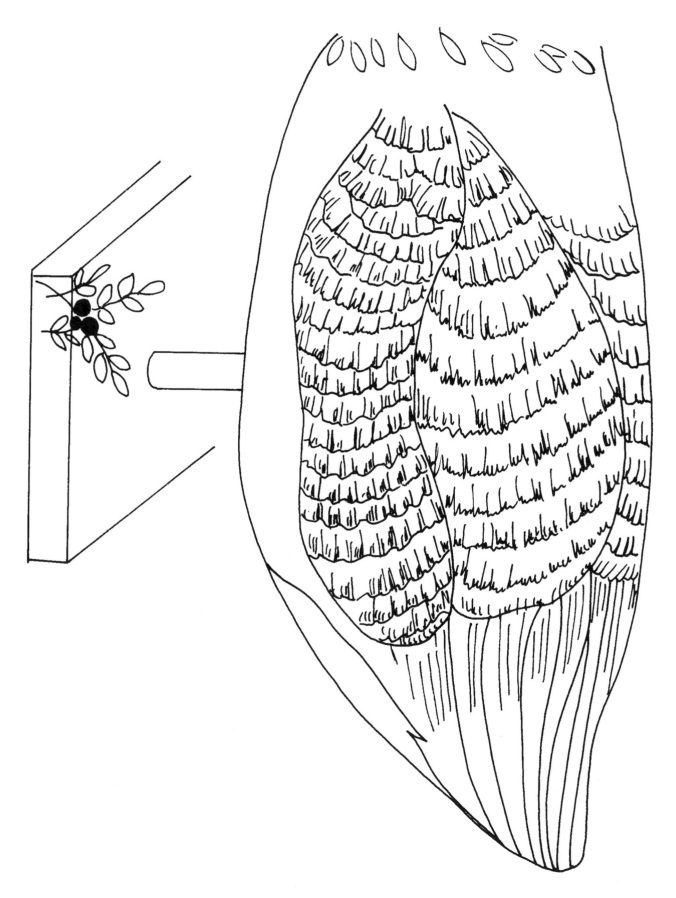

PRETTY POINSETTIA
CUT & PAINTED BOWL

By Laraine Short

SUPPLIES

Decorating Materials:

Basketball gourd, 9-3/4" across

Acrylic craft paint:

Blush flesh
Cadmium yellow
Dark green
Deep burgundy
Jade green
Light green
Limeade
Santa red
Soft peach

Floating medium

Varnish

Tools & Equipment:

Cosmetic sponge

Palette knife

Pencil and eraser

Scissors

Cleaning and cutting tools

Brushes:

Angulars - 1/4", 1/2"
Script liner - 20/0
Stroke - 1"
Deerfoot - 1/4"

PREPARE

1. Clean the gourd and let dry.
2. Transfer top edge of pattern. Cut according to pattern.
3. Sponge gourd with two coats dark green. Let dry.
4. Transfer outline of poinsettia design.

PAINT

Poinsettia:

1. Basecoat with blush flesh, using a 1" stroke brush.
2. Transfer petals.
3. Shade petals with Santa red and highlight with soft peach, using a 1/2" angular brush.
4. Deepen shading with deep burgundy.
5. Thin soft peach with water. Paint veins, using a script liner.
6. Basecoat center of flower with light green and shade with dark green, using a 1/4" angular brush.
7. Stipple centers with cadmium yellow and Santa red, using a 1/4" deerfoot.

Leaves & Vine:

1. Basecoat with jade green, using a 1" stroke brush.
2. Shade with dark green and highlight with limeade, using a 1/2" angular brush.
3. Thin limeade with water and paint veins, using a script liner. Let dry.

FINISH

Brush on two coats of varnish. Let dry. ❑

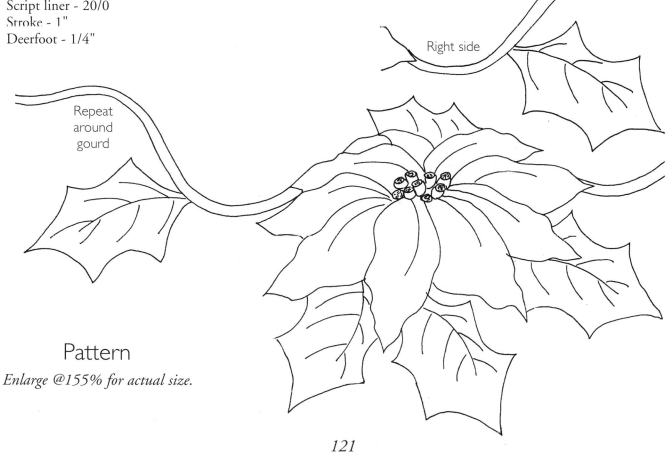

Right side

Repeat around gourd

Pattern

Enlarge @155% for actual size.

SUBTLE POINSETTIA
WOODBURNED BOWL

By Betty Auth

Supplies

Decorating Materials:

Medium round kettle gourd, 7" to 8" in diameter

Leather dyes - Red, green, yellow

Acrylic craft paint - Brown

Waterbase satin varnish

Matte sealer spray

Tools & Equipment:

Cleaning and cutting tools

Woodburning tool

Scissors

Paint brushes - Small rounds, 3/4" flat

Lint-free rags

Patterns
Actual Size

Upper

Lower

Prepare

1. If the gourd has not been cleaned, clean the outside and allow it to dry.
2. Cut off the top of the gourd (the cut height should be 7" to 8"). Clean the inside.
3. Pencil a line all around the rim about 3/8" down from the top edge of the gourd.
4. Transfer the upper poinsettia and leaf design three times, using photo as a guide and spacing the designs evenly around the gourd.
5. Transfer the lower poinsettia and leaf design below each of the first three designs, creating three identical poinsettia sprays.
6. Pencil in a curving, wavy line below the poinsettias all around the bottom of the gourd. (This is where the woodburning will end.)

Burn

1. Go over all the lines with the flow point.
2. Burn scribbled texture over the entire background, burning up to the line around the rim and down to the wavy line at the base.
3. Go back and darken around the poinsettias and leaves.

4. Erase all pencil and graphite from the surface of the gourd.

Color

Color the poinsettias one at a time, beginning with the flower centers. Paint an even – not drippy – coat of leather dye on an area, then blot lightly with the lint-free rag. Add a second coat for deeper color. Paint the flower centers yellow, the flowers red, and the leaves green. Let dry completely.

Finish

1. Apply two coats of satin varnish to the outside of the gourd, allowing to dry between coats.
2. Paint the inside of the gourd brown. Let dry.
3. Spray the inside with matte varnish, taking care not to over-spray on the outside of the gourd. ❑

123

ROLY POLY SNOWMAN
DECORATIVE PAINTED

By Laraine Short

Pattern appears on page 126

SUPPLIES

Decorating Materials:

Bottle gourd, 12" x 8"

Acrylic craft paint:

Burnt umber
Cadmium yellow
Cool white
Orange
Payne's gray
Sable brown
Santa red
Victorian blue
Winter blue

Paperclay *or* air-dry clay (to make nose)

Toothpick (for nose)

6" black felt hat

Fabric strip - 1" x 16" (for hatband)

Glue

Red chalk (for cheeks)

Exterior clear gloss varnish

Raffia

Tools & Equipment:

Cosmetic sponge

Brushes:

Angulars - 3/8", 1/2"
Flat - #16
Script liner - 18/0

PREPARE

1. Sponge gourd with two coats cool white. Occasionally pick up some winter blue. Let dry.
2. Make nose with clay around toothpick, following manufacturer's instructions. Let dry.

PAINT

Face:

1. Basecoat nose with orange. Shade with Santa red. Highlight with cadmium yellow.
2. Transfer pattern for face.
3. Paint eyes with lamp black. Highlight with winter blue. Add reflected light with cool white.
4. Thin lamp black with water and paint mouth.

Coat:

1. Transfer coat pattern (but not the sleeves).
2. Basecoat with Victorian blue. Let dry.
3. Transfer sleeves and arms.
4. Shade coat with Payne's gray.
5. Trim with Santa red.
6. Thin lamp black with water and detail button.

Arms:

1. Basecoat with sable brown.
2. Shade with burnt umber.

FINISH

1. Drill hole for nose. Glue in place.
2. Brush red chalk on cheeks.
3. Brush on two coats of varnish. Let dry.
4. Glue hat in place. Tie fabric around hat. Tie raffia around snowman's neck. ❏

Roly Poly Snowman Pattern
(actual size)
See page 124 for instructions.

METRIC CONVERSION CHART

Inches to Millimeters and Centimeters

Inches	MM	CM
1/8	3	.3
1/4	6	.6
3/8	10	1.0
1/2	13	1.3
5/8	16	1.6
3/4	19	1.9
7/8	22	2.2
1	25	2.5
1-1/4	32	3.2
1-1/2	38	3.8
1-3/4	44	4.4
2	51	5.1
3	76	7.6
4	102	10.2
5	127	12.7
6	152	15.2
7	178	17.8
8	203	20.3
9	229	22.9
10	254	25.4
11	279	27.9
12	305	30.5

Yards to Meters

Yards	Meters
1/8	.11
1/4	.23
3/8	.34
1/2	.46
5/8	.57
3/4	.69
7/8	.80
1	.91
2	1.83
3	2.74
4	3.66
5	4.57
6	5.49
7	6.40
8	7.32
9	8.23
10	9.14

INDEX

continued on next page

INDEX